Living God's Love

An Invitation to Christian Spirituality

GARY HOLLOWAY   EARL LAVENDER

LEAFWOOD
PUBLISHERS

LIVING GOD'S LOVE
An Invitation to Christian Spirituality
published by Leafwood Publishers

Copyright © 2004 by Gary Holloway & Earl Lavender

ISBN 0-9748441-2-8
Printed in the United States of America

Cover design by Greg Jackson

For information:
Leafwood Publishers
1-877-634-6004 (toll free)

Visit our website: www.leafwoodpublishers.com

04 05 06 07 08 09 / 7 6 5 4 3 2 1

To our churches, our colleagues,
and our students who teach us what it
means to live in love with God.

Contents

Introduction

Do you want a deeper relationship with God? A closer walk with Jesus? An inward assurance of the constant presence of the Holy Spirit? Do these statements express the deepest desires of your heart, but you don't know where to begin? Bible study seems so difficult to do consistently. Your prayers seem repetitive and cold. You're not satisfied with your spiritual life, but you don't know where to start to find something better.

This book is for you. It does not offer easy steps, shortcuts, or sure-fire techniques for a deeper spirituality, but it points the way to the path of daily relationship to God. The Bible shows that path, but many of us have not matured beyond our childhood misconceptions of God and our relationship to him. For us and for those young in Christian experience, much of the vocabulary and practices of Christian spirituality are new.

This book is therefore by beginners for beginners. To admit we are beginners in our walk with God is not to deny the reality of the relationship we have enjoyed with him for years. Instead, it is to stand at the threshold of a deeper, fuller path to God. Like Dorothy in Oz, the landscape will seem both familiar and new. We will rediscover what we have known before—Bible study, prayer, fellowship, and service—but in deeper and richer ways. If these ways seem strange—and they seemed strange to us at first—at least give them a chance and an honest try.

But like all relational journeys, the path will bring both joy and struggle. The path we journey through the Spirit, with Jesus, to our home with God is not the yellow-brick road, but the dusty path to Calvary. It is a road that requires self-sacrifice, discipline, and consistency. It is also the way of inexpressible joy, for the God of love travels with us. This is an invitation into the very heart of God.

Learning to travel that road to God is much like learning to jog (see 1 Corinthians 9:24-26; 1 Timothy 4:7-10; Hebrews 12:1-13). We first need motivation—better health, loss of weight, time to be with friends, a picture of what we would like to be. Spiritually we need an image of what God wants us to be. But why do we need to learn how to jog? We have been running all our lives! Because jogging is more intentional, regular, disciplined running. Likewise, we also have been praying all our lives but we need more regular, disciplined prayer.

One does not learn to jog by reading books (although books may help). To learn to run, you must begin to run. It's the same with spiritual practices. What helps most in jogging is a good coach and helpful running partners. Spiritually, we never run alone. Jesus runs with us through the Holy Spirit, and we run together with fellow believers. Jogging consistently means discipline, running daily even when we do not feel like it. Spiritual practices are also not always fun, but require consistency even when boring and painful. No pain, no gain.

But in jogging and in our journey to God, there is great gain. The path of this journey begins with the God who pursues us in love. That loving God will be our focus throughout this book. Spiritual practices have little value without centering on God. From there the path flows into God's action in his kingdom and his call to personal relationship. We then discuss listening to God and communicating with him in prayer as ways of strengthening that relationship. This loving relationship with him requires regular practices to help us grow in love. That relationship takes place in community. As we walk with God, we must avoid rivals to his love. Finally, love for God always overflows to genuine love and service to others. This is our journey with God.

We make this journey together. God is always *our* Father. This book itself is the product of a community of faith. The authors write jointly; so much so that we usually use "I," not "we," to refer to ourselves in the book. Others shared helpful insights along the way. We particularly thank Deb Holloway, Rebecca Lavender, Melanee Bandy, Cindy Kinnie, Rosalind Powell, George Johnson, Mike Ripski, John York, Mark Black, Lee Camp, George Goldman, Phillip Camp, Steve Sherman, John Mark Hicks, Mike Williams, Terry Briley, and Carl McKelvey for their wisdom. Most of all we trust and pray that God has been at work in our writing and will work powerfully in you as you read.

God lives and works in community. That is why this book will be of more value if you study and practice in small groups. There are questions and practices at the end of each chapter for individuals, but also for group work from the beginning of this process. God works through others to draw us to himself. That's why groups are so important.

But whether you begin by yourself, with a small group, or a larger group or class, the important thing is to begin. God invites you into relationship with him, just as you are. Even if you're not sure about God, even if you have no religious background, even if you've been a faithful churchgoer all your life, God invites you to share his very life, a life richer than you can imagine.

Part 1

LIVING IN GOD'S LOVE

Father, Son, and Spirit invite us into the
relationship they share. The story of that relationship
is told in the Bible, which is also our story. God calls
us to live in that relationship of love, to live a new
life in the kingdom of God.

CHAPTER ONE

A God Who Loves

Who is God to you right now? What word first pops into your mind when you hear, "God"? How would you picture God?

You might respond that you really don't picture God at all. "God" might just be a word to you, with little specific content. You might take God for granted. He is a convenient God who helps you when you want him. Or your God may be a distant God who did great things in Bible times and is up there somewhere watching over things, but not active in today's world, much less in the daily struggles of your life. Perhaps your God is a "religious" God, found in churches, active on Sunday, but far removed from the office during the week. He is an out-of-date God who doesn't understand contemporary life.

Perhaps you have an angry, demanding God. No matter what you do, you feel his disapproval. You can never be good enough for him, but still you try. Talk of God makes you feel guilty. You don't love him enough, do enough for him, or care as much about other people as he wants you to.

Or you might be angry at God, thinking he has a lot to answer for. God to you is the tyrant who allows others to abuse you. He can cure cancer, stop war, and feed the hungry, but for some reason he will not. Or maybe he wants to but simply can't. He's a nice God, but powerless.

It may be that all of these images of God flow through our hearts at different times. Why bring this up? Isn't this a book about spirituality? Why begin with talk of God? Must we fully understand God before we are spiritual?

Of course not. But this book is not about generic spirituality, but about relationship to God. We define spirituality as "the mysterious process of God at work in us." As mystery, we cannot fully explain this process. God cannot be fully explained, but he can be genuinely experienced. And so we ask, who is this God at work in us? What kind of God is he?

An Active God Who Pursues Us in Love

In the Bible, God reveals his true character (that's why we sometimes refer to Scripture as "special revelation"). God pulls back the thick curtain of our misconceptions to walk boldly onto the stage of history and make himself known. From Genesis to Revelation, the picture of God is consistent. He is a God who loves his creation forever. He created all things out of love. He lovingly molded humans from the ground, breathed life into them, and made them in his image (Genesis 1:27; 2:7).

But we humans soon rejected the love of God, preferring our own desires to his, wanting to be our own gods (Genesis 3:1-7). But even so, God does not reject us. He continues to pursue humanity in love. Enoch, Noah, Abraham, Sarah, Moses, Rahab, Samuel, David—all are beloved by God.

Yet it is not only the "heroes" of Scripture that God loves. His love is for everyone, even those who hunger for him in ignorance of who he really is. From creation, people have hungered for God, because he made us for himself. God alone can satisfy our deepest longings, but we try to satisfy them in countless ways. We pursue pleasure, success, security, wealth, romance, and numerous other ways to fill the deep longing within. We worship other gods.

God clearly condemns idolatry, but does not condemn that craving for something to make us whole. Indeed, when Paul goes to Athens, the city that epitomized the best of culture in his day, he finds it full of idols. Asked to speak about his God in front of a group of philosophers, Paul does not condemn their hunger for gods, but praises it. Having found an altar inscribed "To An Unknown God," he says, "Now what you worship as something unknown I am going to proclaim to you" (Acts 17:23).

The God Paul proclaims is the loving God who made heaven and earth. He created humans so he could have relationship with them. "God did this so that men would seek him and perhaps reach out for him and find him, though he is not far from each one of us" (Acts 17:27). Paul then quotes, not the Bible, but pagan poets who say, "'For in him we live and move and have our being.' As some of your own poets have said, 'We are his offspring'" (Acts 17:28).

So what's wrong with paganism? It's not simply that these idolaters are wrong about God. What is devastating is that their erroneous view of God kept them from fully embracing his love. Although they do not know it, these idol worshippers are beloved children of God.

Our God is not distant, angry, or powerless. He is a God who is near to us, near to all. He wants us to come close to him in love. He became one of us in Jesus to captivate us with gentle, endearing words, and self-sacrificing acts. At our births, he placed within each of us a hunger for happiness, wholeness, and meaning. A hunger for him. God loves and wants you for his own.

A Trinity of Love

This God reveals himself as a Trinity. It is not necessary for us to fathom the Trinity completely. We cannot, for he is the ultimate mystery. We cannot define God, but we can find him. We are invited into a relationship with the Trinity, a God who reveals his love for us in three ways.

God is a loving Father. He is the Father of all in creation ("we are his offspring") and our Father through his Son Jesus Christ. As Christians, we are as much the beloved sons and daughters of God as Jesus himself. God loves us as much as he loves Jesus. One of the great expressions of God's love for Jesus came at his baptism. When Jesus is baptized, the heavens open, the Spirit descends, and a voice speaks, "You are my Son, whom I love; with you I am well pleased" (Mark 1:10-11).

What we may not realize is that what happened to Jesus at his baptism also happened to us. When we were baptized, the heavens opened. No barriers stood between God and us. He removed the curtain of our sin, ignorance, and unbelief and showed himself to us. When we were baptized, the Spirit descended on us. God himself through his Holy Spirit now lives within us and makes us his. Most amazingly of all, when we were baptized, God said, "You are my son, my daughter, whom I love. I am pleased with you!"

And what had Jesus done to deserve to be called the beloved Son of God? What do you mean, "What had he done?" He didn't have to do anything; he simply was the Son of God. Exactly. And so are we. We are children of God by birth and new birth. We have not earned our status, but God freely gives it. God is a Father who loves his children unconditionally.

But what happens when we spurn God's love? Do we then forfeit our standing as his children? Does God quit loving us when we refuse to love him? No. The story of the prodigal son shows that even when we abandon him, he waits patiently for our return, keeping robe, ring, and fatted calf prepared. He meets our return not with an angry face and a cold acceptance, but with loving arms and a warm embrace (see Luke 15:11-32). God is always our loving Father.

God became flesh in Jesus Christ. Jesus is the great teacher of love, the human face of the love of God. "For God so loved the world that he gave his one and only Son, that whoever believes in him shall not perish but have eternal life. For God did not send his Son into the world to condemn the world, but to save the world through him" (John 3:16-17). Jesus reveals the face of a loving God who wants us for his own, not one who condemns.

As the great teacher of love, Jesus gave his followers the command to love each other, to love those in the world, and even to love their enemies. But Jesus came not just to command that we love, but to show us how. He calls us to be his students, his disciples, his apprentices who learn from him, our teacher and master. He came to show us what it means to live in God's love, to realize his love for us, and to show his love to others. From Jesus, we learn how to love God through hearing his word, through prayer, through service, and through sacrifice.

But our relationship with Jesus is more dynamic than simply following his example. It is more than asking, "What would Jesus do?" As we will see in following chapters, we not only learn to pray like Jesus, but he prays in and with us. We do serve others like Jesus because he continues powerfully to serve through us. We love because his love flows through us. God the Son loves in us.

So the spirituality we explore in this book, the mysterious work of God in us, is Christian spirituality. We are not concerned with spirituality in general without concern for the content of spirituality. Its content is the embodied life of God in Jesus and in us. God works in us through Jesus. To be spiritual then is to follow Christ, to be his disciple, to seek his kingdom. We do not know how to love God or neighbor except through Christ who lives in us.

God is a Holy Spirit who transforms us in love. God loved us so much that he sent his only Son to give us eternal life. But Jesus did more for us than simply save us from our sins. He promised his disciples a new Helper, the Holy Spirit, would be with them after he went back to his Father (John 14:15-18). Jesus did not abandon us as his followers, leaving us to do our best without him. Instead, he continues to live and love within us through the Holy Spirit.

God loves and accepts us just as we are, but in his love he does not leave us just as we are. He and Jesus make their home in us through the Spirit, and through the Spirit their love transforms us. This is what we mean by words like "holy," "sanctification," and "saint." God loves us so much that as we live in his love, following Jesus as disciples, we become more like him. We share in his nature, more and more becoming love as he is love.

God is love. The significance of the Trinity for spirituality is that God's very nature is relationship. Even before he created, God has always existed in the loving relationship between Father, Son, and Spirit. God therefore invites to share in this dynamic relationship, to love as he is love. He draws us into his very life.

In this book, we will talk about different ways we can open our hearts and lives to receive the love of God. But we should never think of these practices as "good works" we do. They do not make us superior to others. They do not make us worthy of God's love. Instead, these practices allow God to work in us through his Holy Spirit. They are "spiritual" practices, not because they are mysterious, religious, inner, or sacred (although they may be all of these things), but because they come from the Holy Spirit of God, the Spirit of love.

God's Invitation to Love

Many Christians may use spiritual disciplines and practices as techniques to make themselves better, holier, and more spiritual. They forget that God gives us these practices so we may seek him. It is God we want, not religion, spirituality, meaning, or even happiness. But to truly desire to "seek the face of God" (Psalm 24:6), we must be assured that he is seeking us. God wants us more than we want him. The eternal, almighty Father, Son, and Spirit deeply desire a relationship with us. That is why we begin a book on spirituality with an extended discussion of God's love.

That relationship is much like a romance. God does not choose to rule us with an iron fist. He does not set demanding standards for his approval. He does not condemn. He invites. He tries to win us over. He only asks to love and cherish us. For our own good he asks our love in return. "Taste and see that the Lord is good" (Psalm 34:8).

If the idea of falling in love with God sounds strange to you, remember the Bible frequently describes the relationship between God and his people this way. The Old Testament speaks of God pursuing his beloved Israel with gentle words of intimacy, "Therefore I am now going to allure her; I will lead her into the desert and speak tenderly to her" (Hosea 2:14, see also Isaiah 62:5; Jeremiah 2:2; Ezekiel 16:8). God even invites his people to call him their husband: "In that day," declares the Lord, "you will call me 'my husband'; you will no longer call me 'my master'" (Hosea 2:16).

Jesus uses the language of romance when he calls himself our husband and us his bride (see Matthew 9:15; Mark 2:19; John 3:29). Paul and John also use this romantic, relational, marriage imagery (Romans 7:1-4; 2 Corinthians 11:2; Ephesians 5:22-33; Revelation 19:7; 21:2, 9; 22:17). If we are uncomfortable with this biblical image of romance with God, perhaps we need to examine the depth of our relationship with him. His love for us is stronger than the love of any husband for his wife or wife for her husband.

Christian spirituality is falling in love with the God we see in Christ. That mysterious process of God lovingly at work in us is not a trick, a shortcut, or a technique. It is a way of life. It is believing from the heart, the very center of our being, believing that God loves us. It is living in that place of deep trust and acceptance.

We do not live in that place alone. Not only are we with God, but with others in love. That is why life in community is so important to Christian spirituality. The practices discussed later in this book are not merely for individuals but are always also group practices. There is no Lone Ranger Christian spirituality. Jesus teaches us that even when we go into our private place to be alone with God, we pray not to "my Father" but to "our Father."

This is why small groups are so essential to spiritual growth. While one can read and follow this book by oneself, it will be much more helpful if practiced in small groups.

Our relationship with a loving God is not always an easy one. Just as in human relationships, the closer we get to God the greater the pain and the greater the joy. Jesus calls us to take up our crosses and die so we can share his glory. Through the Spirit, we put to death the deeds of the body so we may have life (Romans 8:13). Know up front that Christian spirituality is not easy. We might even be afraid that loving God is too hard and demanding.

It is demanding. God wants all that we are. There is no corner of our hearts and lives he does not desire. But he desires them because it is truly good for us. Ultimately, he does not want to fix us, reform us, or merely save us from hell. Instead, he wants to receive us, accept us, and love us.

All this talk of God's love is not meant simply to make us feel good about ourselves. It is meant to invite us into a life of love. Answering that call will demand our time, effort, and discipline. We should think twice before beginning a more intentional journey of discipleship. But at the end of that long road is a God who loves us. Although we may not always feel him near, he is with us, not just at the end but every step of the way.

We need to look for him at every step. It is helpful to review your life journey so far. Take some time to reflect on how God has constantly pursued you. Look for him in those mountaintop experiences and in times of doubt and despair. Think of the turning points of your life. Was God there? Did you sense him at work? Were you looking? Did you see him at church? In friends? In prayer? In the beauty of the world? In your darkest hour? Have you experienced the absence of God?

Perhaps even now you do not feel him near. Perhaps God still seems distant, angry, or powerless to you. You may feel far from him. You may not feel like God's beloved son or daughter. What should you do?

The invitation from God still stands. He still wants you whether you feel he does or not. The first step is to act as though God loves you even if you're not fully convinced he does. If you follow the spiritual practices discussed in this book with the intent of seeking God, then you can act yourself into a new way of being. Faith and feeling will follow if you take God up on his offer of love and relationship. In the words of Therese of Lisieux, "Jesus does not demand great deeds, but only gratitude and self-surrender."

For Personal Reflection

1. Write down the names you use most often for God. What do they tell you about your relationship to God? What name for God do you use in prayer? How would you describe God?

2. Where did you get your view of God? Parents? Church? Sunday School? The Bible? Television? Cartoons? Are those views adequate?

3. What is your reaction to the concept of a romance with God? Why do you react that way? What does your reaction say about your view of God?

4. Can you make yourself love God? Can you act yourself into a new way of being? What's the use of practicing spirituality if you don't feel spiritual?

Going Deeper

1. Using crayons or colored markers, draw a picture of God. What do you learn about your view of God from this picture? If you think this is a childish exercise, ask yourself, "Has my view of God changed significantly from my childhood?" If so, how?

2. Write a brief spiritual autobiography. How has God pursued you through the years? How has he shown his love? How have you sought him?

Group Work

1. If you do not already belong to a small group that seeks God, begin to pray that God will send you three or four fellow seekers so you may form a group. Listen closely in those prayers. God does not always send who we might expect.

2. Each time you meet in your small group, but especially the first time, it is important to remind the group of your purposes for meeting. Your ultimate purpose for meeting is not friendship, sup-

port, or therapy, but to help each other be open to the work of God in your lives. The group should prayerfully commit itself to that intention, to strict confidentiality concerning what is shared in the group, and to listening to one another without condemnation. In short, the golden rule is the rule for small groups.

3. Once you form the small group, have each member read this chapter. Then share with one another the pictures you drew of God (#1 in Going Deeper). What do others see in your picture? What does that say about God or your view of God?

4. Share with one another when you feel closest to God in nature. What landscape, weather, animals, and plants move you closer to God? Why? What does that say about your view of God?

For Further Reading

For Beginners

Peace, Richard. *Spiritual Autobiography: Discovering and Sharing Your Spiritual Story.* Colorado Springs: NavPress, 1998.

Reading Deeper

Curtis, Brent, and Eldredge, John. *The Sacred Romance: Drawing Closer to the Heart of God.* Nashville: Thomas Nelson, 1997.

Hagberg, Janet O. and Guelich, Robert A. *The Critical Journey: Stages in the Life of Faith.* Salem, Wisconsin: Sheffield Publishing, 1989.

Nouwen, Henri J.M. *Making All Things New.* San Francisco: Harper, 1981.

Spiritual Classics

Kelly, Thomas R. *A Testament of Devotion.* San Francisco: Harper, 1941.

Teresa of Avila. *A Life of Prayer.* Edited by James H. Houston. Minneapolis: Bethany House, 1998.

CHAPTER TWO

Life in the Kingdom of Love

When you fall in love, you want to share the life of your beloved. It's true that when you marry you marry not just an individual but an entire family. More than that, you become part of the heritage of the one you love. All that shapes her becomes part of you. His story becomes your story.

So also when we fall in love with God. Sharing in the life of God is what makes spirituality "Christian." Is "spirituality" a general category with "Christian" as a specific type? No. Some may want a general spirituality that improves life, leading to self-actualization and self-awareness. For them, something like Transcendental Meditation will do. Christian spirituality, however, is uniquely centered in a relationship with God—Father, Son, and Spirit—and relationships with others through God. Falling in love with the Almighty Ruler of the Universe means we participate in the very life of God. In him, our lives take on a cosmic significance. The Bible tells the story of our relationship with the God who reigns over everything, often describing this cluster of spiritual relationships as "the kingdom of God."

God's Invitation to Kingdom Living

Out of his wonderful love, God invites us to live in his kingdom, to surrender willingly to his reign, to live in that place where his will is done. That surrender to God is no defeat for us, since God's kingdom is the only place where we can live to the fullest. God created us to enjoy abundant life. This is not self-actualization or a "name it, claim it" gospel. It is not living successfully according to the fallen standards of our world. Instead, this is living a purposeful life in relationship with God and others. This is the good news that Jesus announced: we can live under the reign of God. "The time has come," he said. "The kingdom of God is near. Repent and believe the good news!" (Mark 1:15). But if we do not understand the nature of God's loving invitation into his kingdom, we will miss the abundant life found there. Learning to live life in its fullest expression in relationship with our Creator is the purpose of genuine spiritual formation.

How does "church" relate to kingdom? The church is to be a colony of God's kingdom in our world. But not everything done by churches or every group that calls itself a church truly participates or lives in the kingdom. The kingdom of God is anywhere God's will is done (see Matthew 6:10). A church comprised of authentic believers who have submitted their lives to God is a true manifestation of the kingdom. Those in that church are living according to God's will and enjoying his gracious guidance. Once again, God's kingdom is where his will is being done, where God lives his love through us.

Living under God's direction answers the age-old question, "Why are we here?" God created us in his image and his likeness (Genesis 1:26). He made us to be like him, made us for relationship. In creation, God gave humans the most exalted role, to represent and even share in the character and person of God himself. Those who choose this life under God's direction embody God's kingdom. They serve as God's ambassadors, calling others to the joys of relationship with God.

Life in the Kingdom: A Six-Act Story

The Bible is the fascinating and dynamic story of a loving God interacting with his creatures in a gracious way in spite of their rebellion. Unfortunately, for many believers the biblical stories remain isolated in a distant past, far removed from their daily lives. But Christian spirituality requires embracing the biblical story as our story. Not just the creation story, but all the stories of the Bible are about God's loving relationship with humanity. With us!

We therefore live in the biblical story; it becomes the story of our lives. Thus, the main character in my autobiography is not me, but God. He alone gives my life meaning. The same is true of you. The Bible story is our story because it is the story of God. He is the hero of every Bible story. When we look at the accounts of Israel long ago, they are not merely ancient documents or old Sunday School lessons. They are living stories of our own lives. This is why Bible study is so important. In the Bible we meet God and we meet our true selves.

Some compare human history as told in the Bible to an unfinished six-act play.[1] The play begins happily since **Act One is creation**. The creation story in the first three chapters of Genesis reveals humanity's purpose. After lovingly creating humans in his image, God placed them in a beautiful garden and willingly supplied their every need. He called them to care for the garden, to rule over living things, to multiply and fill the earth, and to exercise dominion—all activities of God himself. Humans were to exercise dominion over the world not in a careless and selfish way, but in the loving, caring way God rules his world.

Not only did God give directions on how to live, he also set limits, giving humans opportunity to choose freely to obey him.

God told them not to eat of the fruit of the tree of the knowledge of good and evil. To do so would be presumptuous, a clear claim that they did not need to be subject to God and his guidance. By eating the forbidden fruit, they declared autonomy from the God who made them, breaking relationship with him and refusing to live in his kingdom.

But why did God test humanity this way? Why would a God of love place us in a situation where he knew we would fail him? How could a good God put the creatures he had created for relationship, his own image-bearers, at risk? Because he is love. Love, by definition, must be free. A forced love is no love at all. If there were no alternative to following and loving God, then our responding love would not be authentic, and Christian spirituality is all about authentic loving relationship with God. God so wants us to have a meaningful and intimate relationship with him that he allows us the possibility of rejecting him.

Tragically, given the choice, humans rebelled against God's invitation to love him and submit to his will. **This tragic fall of humanity from God's purposes is Act Two of the story**. The Bible calls that rejection of God's love "sin." But even after the fall into sin, we see the merciful love of God. God could have given up on humanity since we had rejected him, the source of life, but instead God gave life again. It was life greatly affected by the seriousness of sin, a life full of difficulty and eventually death, but it was still a merciful opportunity to live. Although we rejected him, God had a plan to reconcile us to him in love. What should have been the end of the story was just the beginning. The story was now not simply one of a loving Creator, but of a reconciling Father whose never-failing love seeks to restore us to him.

The fall introduced a kingdom in competition to God's, the kingdom of self-rule. That doesn't sound too bad, does it? The kingdom of self-rule? Isn't self-reliance one of our culture's chief values? After all, how bad can eating the fruit of self-determination actually be? Here we see the sly deception of one who desperately wants to defeat the plans and purposes of God. In the Genesis story, he is a serpent. The Bible usually calls this deceiver Satan. To defeat us, Satan doesn't require our overt allegiance to his kingdom. All he has to do is to turn us away from God by convincing us that life is about our glory and our kingdom. Satan is not even disturbed if we worship God on occasion as long as we live in a world of our making rather than in submission to God's will.

With Adam and Eve, it wasn't so much "eating the fruit" that brought such disastrous consequences. It was the sin motivating the eating of the fruit. "You will be like God," the serpent told Eve (Genesis 3:5). Humans ever since have presumed they were gods instead of God's. It's not so much individual sins that separate us from God, but the deliberate walking away from God's intent for us. Like Adam and Eve, each of us turns from the blessed life in the beautiful garden of God's kingdom to embrace harsh toil in a world of our own making.

And so the story continues for us to this day. God created each of us to be like God so we could glorify him. To that end, God gave us the freedom to have a genuine relationship with him and with others. It was also the freedom to rebel against him, set our own path, and eat the forbidden fruit of self-governance. We turn from the offer of life directed by our Creator and set out on our own to attempt to live counter to God's purposes.

God's relationship with Israel is Act Three of the biblical story. God had a plan to reconcile humanity to him in spite of its rebellion. That plan was to become human himself in Jesus Christ. To prepare for the coming of one person, Jesus, God prepared an entire people, Israel. God chose them through Abraham, delivered them from slavery in Egypt, and made a covenant (a formal statement of relationship) with them at Sinai. God offered himself to them as their loving Father provided they would be loyal to him alone (Exodus 20:2-6). Israel was thus to be God's kingdom, the place where his will was done.

However, although the Israelites had this good news proclaimed to them, they did not accomplish their intended purpose
in God's plan (see Hebrews 4:1-5). This is not to downplay those
who were faithful throughout Israel's history, for there were many,
but to recognize that God had a wonderful purpose for Israel—
tremendously good news—from which she, as a nation, turned
away. In the same way, since Israel's story is part of our story, we
also can miss the point of the good news from God. Good news here
is more than the death of Jesus on the cross so we might have life
after death. It is the good news that through Jesus we have the
opportunity to live in God's kingdom now. The purpose of Jesus
was to give us the gift of living as God originally intended, not to
forgive us of sins and "save us" to continue to live in self-centered
rebellion. Even Christian spirituality can be twisted into a technique
for personal happiness instead of the long path of obedience.

This is why we must never lose focus on the name and work
of Jesus. To do so is to reject the amazing offer of God to enter his
kingdom. Though God delivered us, like Israel, from the slavery
to self, we (like them) can refuse to enter the gracious rest of his
kingdom.

The purpose of spiritual growth is to know God's will in a
deeper and more compelling way so that we might more fully realize the life for which he created us. Spirituality will enhance the
self, but only in relationship with God. Thus as we consider the
story of Israel's failure as a nation to accept God's loving invitation,
we must ask ourselves if we too are guilty of the same self-centered
rebellion against God's purposes for us. Their story is our story.

What were God's purposes for Israel? His loving call was for
them to be a light to the nations around them, so that all might
know him. He invited them to take a leading part in his plan to
reconcile the world to himself, to proclaim the kingdom of God for
all. However, they misunderstood God's purpose in choosing
them, believing it was all about them, not about God. They participated in required religious ritual, but lived self-focused lives.

They disregarded the offer to live in God's kingdom because they wanted to expand their own self-rule.

Ezekiel 36 provides interesting insight into Israel's rejection of God's purposes for them. God called them to proclaim his holy name to the nations. Instead, they profaned his name by choosing to live like the nations around them, living self-focused, worldly lives. The rich lived in blatant disregard of the poor. Some had food to eat in abundance while others starved. Because of their rebellion, God sent Israel into captivity, but he did not abandon his people. If we reject the awesome love of God, he does not reject us. He does all he can to invite us into his love. So for the sake of his holy name, God promised a new covenant.

The story of that new covenant is the story of Jesus, Act Four of the story. "For God so loved the world that he gave his only Son..." (John 3:16). Even in humanity's constant refusal to submit to him, God took the ultimate step to reconcile us to himself. He sent his only Son as the embodiment of the life for which he created us. In Jesus, the exact representation of God, the eternal purposes of God became flesh and lived among us (John 1:1, 14; Hebrews 1:1-3). Jesus announced the arrival of God's kingdom in a fuller form. He himself embodied the rule of God, saying, "The kingdom of God is among you" (Luke 17:21).

In his death on the cross, Jesus showed the depth of God's love for us. "While we were still sinners, Christ died for us" (Romans 5:8). This is the length to which God will go to win us back. By his death, Jesus reconciles us to God and brings us into God's kingdom. By his resurrection from the dead, Jesus demonstrates his power over all evil. Jesus, as the embodiment of the kingdom, lovingly invites us to walk with him there.

Those who accept that invitation to walk with Jesus make up the church, which is Act Five of the story. As we read the story of the early church in the Bible, it is not a matter of joining the right group, but all about being a disciple, a pupil, of Jesus, following him step by step in kingdom life. Even that does not adequately express the dynamic nature of our relationship with God through Christ. Jesus ascended back to God the Father, but he did not abandon us. He sent us his Spirit. Thus, we do not merely imitate Jesus, asking, "What would Jesus do?" as if we could be like him on our own power. No. Instead, Jesus himself lives in us through his Holy Spirit.

So the story of the church is the continuing story of Jesus in the world, embodied in our flesh and blood. That's why the church is often called the body of Christ. Jesus himself along with the Father make their home in us (John 14:23). We therefore can say, "I no longer live, but Christ lives in me" (Galatians 2:20). Such a total surrender to Jesus does not mean he obliterates our personalities. Instead, it is only in union with Christ that we embody God's kingdom and become truly ourselves, all we were meant to be.

We live out the will of God in relationship with him and with others. We will talk later of this life in community, but that is what God means by "church." The church is not an institution but a living, breathing relationship. As church, we become spiritual friends with one another and with God. Since God is Trinity, he has never been alone. To share in God's life means we too are never alone. Christian spirituality is both personal and communal.

This also means the great play of time has not yet ended. We live in the unfinished fifth act, waiting for Act Six. We are not the only ones to live in that unfinished fifth act. The story of God's presence in human history continues after the writing of the Bible, particularly in the lives of those in relationship with him. That's why we can learn more of how to follow God from those faithful to him in the past. Their story is also part of God's story and our story. The kingdom of God stretches throughout space and time to embrace all those in every age and every country who live out God's will.

However, the story of history is not merely a script we follow, but a play God co-writes with us. Life is real and earnest. Out of love, our Father invites us to live the fullest life possible, a life in him. And so in light of the first four Acts of the story, God lives in us in this fifth act, improvising each day the happiest ending there can possibly be.

That end is Act Six, the return of Jesus, what the Bible calls the eschaton or "last things." Some Christians become distracted by speculations on how the world will end. However, the point of eschatology is not that the world as we know it will end, but that God has an end (or purpose) in mind for his creation, an end he is working toward even now. Thus, the church does not simply have eschatology, a theory about how the world ends, but rather embodies eschatology, living out the new creation purposes of God.

Because we know what God will one day accomplish—he will make all things new and bring righteousness, justice and peace— then we as his faithful children should be actively involved in bringing about these things now. The sixth act of God's drama of redemption is not just a future dream; it provides direction and purpose for our lives as we continue to live in the "fifth act."

That means God's kingdom is both now and not yet. Now we embody Jesus, but we look forward to that day when we see him with our own eyes. This will be the climax of life in the kingdom of God, the never-ending day when we see God, our beloved, face-to-face. There he will wipe away every tear from our eyes, and we will live eternally in a renewed heaven and earth with the one who is Love himself (Revelation 21:1-5, 22-27). Falling in love with God is not just for a lifetime, but forever.

Embracing the Reign of Love

Why spend so much time on the biblical story in a book on Christian spirituality? Don't we know the story? Is spirituality simply knowing about the Bible?

No, it is much more. But in a world full of competing "spiritualities," it is important to clarify what makes Christian spirituality unique. Christian spirituality is a lived relationship with the

God revealed in the Bible. He is a God with a story, a history with humanity. He made us, pursued us, and even died for us. He wants to be our God and for us to be his people. He wants to rule our lives in love, for our own good. That's the beauty of the kingdom of God.

God through Christ invites us to embrace his love for us. This is the grand invitation of Jesus, not just to be part of a church or to be "saved." Rather, Jesus came not just to save us from our sins but also to save us for himself. He invites us to be his disciples, to embrace love even though it means going to the cross, following him step by step into kingdom life. "Come to me, you who are weary and burdened, and I will give you rest. Take my yoke on you and learn of me, for I am meek and humble in heart, and you will find rest for your souls. My yoke is easy and my burden is light" (Matthew 11:29). This is the greatest invitation.

The path of spiritual formation is to dedicate our lives to being authentic followers of Jesus, so we might learn the walk for which we were made. This invitation calls for a decisive step into the kingdom of God. We can only accept it through the one who is "the way, the truth and the life" (John 14:6). God's magnificent gift awaits, the good news blasts out like the sound of a trumpet, "The kingdom of God is at hand." Hear the invitation. Start on the path. Embrace the kingdom of love.

For Personal Reflection

1. How do you view the biblical story? Do you see yourself in the story as part of God's redemptive plan? If so, how does that shape your life today?

2. What does "kingdom of God" mean to you? Do you find Jesus' invitation into the kingdom compelling? Why or why not?

3. Why do you think Israel misunderstood God's purpose for them? How can we avoid the same mistake?

4. What gets you out of bed in the morning? Do you see your work as something that allows you to get by, or as an opportunity to embody God's kingdom?

Going Deeper

1. Take a few minutes each day to reflect in writing on where you saw God working in your life that day. This can be the beginning of a daily spiritual journal (see Chapter Six for more on journaling).

2. Begin each day this week by intentionally acknowledging that the only purpose for you that day is to embody the kingdom of God.

If this beginning makes a significant difference in your day, reflect on this in your personal journal.

3. Set regular reminders throughout the day of God's calling for you to embody the life of Christ in all you do and say.

Group Work

1. List the five most important things you think God wants you to do in your lifetime. Share your list with the group. What items do you have in common? What does this say about your understanding of the purpose and direction of your life?

2. What changes in the activities of your church need to be made to help you accomplish what God wants you to do?

3. What is accountability? Develop ways to hold one another accountable for intentionally living each day in God's kingdom. Discuss what difference this accountability makes in your daily activities.

For Further Reading

For Beginners

Norris, Gunilla. *Being Home: Discovering the Spiritual in the Everyday.*
　　Mahwah, New Jersey: HiddenSpring, 2001.

Reading Deeper

Barry, William A. *Finding God in All Things.* Notre Dame: Ave
　　Maria Press, 1991.
Willard, Dallas. *The Divine Conspiracy: Discovering our Hidden
　　Life in God.* San Francisco: Harper, 1998.

Spiritual Classics

Guyon, Madame. *Experiencing the Depths of Jesus Christ.* Nashville:
　　Thomas Nelson, 2000.

Note

1. The "six acts" of the biblical story is borrowed from J. Richard
Middleton and Brian Walsh, *Truth is Stranger Than It Used to Be* (Downers
Grove, IL: InterVarsity Press, 1995) 182. Many other scholars have suggested
similar divisions of the biblical drama.

CHAPTER THREE

Beginning a Relationship with God

In any relationship, growth will not occur without commitment. In romance there are different levels of commitment. After dating for a while, we might commit to "going steady," to an exclusive dating relationship. In time, that might blossom into engagement, a commitment to marry. Then there is the big one, the marriage ceremony itself, where we promise in front of God and witnesses to be faithful to this one person for the rest of our lives. Even after marriage, there are reminders of our commitment, perhaps marked by some kind of special ceremony.

There is also a progression in our commitment to God. Somewhere along the line, many of us have pledged that commitment in a cluster of ceremonies that goes by many names—"conversion," "accepting Jesus," and "being born again."

This chapter may convince you to take that step of commitment. However, most readers of this book have already committed their lives to God through Christ. So why talk of events that are in the past? "Have you been born again?" we ask people. "Yes," they reply, "I have been born again."

Wouldn't it be better if we changed our language about conversion to make it more like our language about another permanent commitment, marriage? You ask me, "Are you married?" I reply, "I have been married." What kind of impression would that answer give? Wouldn't you think me widowed or (more likely) divorced? Now the truth is I have been married. It's been a long time since my wedding and my memories are hazy regarding that event, but I assure you, I have been married by a preacher and before witnesses. My answer, "I have been married," is therefore true.

True, but misleading. It's not just that I have been through a marriage ceremony, but more importantly, that I am married. Happily so, in case you wonder. Those vows I made many years ago changed my identity. I am now my wife's husband. Two became one. Those vows brought me into a new family.

It's the same way with new birth. It's true that we who are Christians have been born again. True, but misleading. It makes it sound as if our conversion was some ritual in our past that has little meaning for us now. It would be better if we said, "I am born again." Born with Jesus. In his Name. Into his death. United with his resurrection. Our commitment is once and for all. There we made our vows to cling to him alone. We became united with him. We came into a new family. Forever. Even if it means we go to the cross with him. And we will. But these vows not even death can sever.

The Beginning of Relationship

God becomes the focus in people's lives in many different ways. Some grew up hearing about their loving God and his will for them. They have never really felt estranged from him. As they mature, they come to more fully understand the incredible love of God who loves them in spite of their sinfulness. Others have lived very difficult lives away from God, but found him in their adult years. Still others lived easy lives of self-focused comfort with no thought of or desire for God, only to find him when their lives fell apart. But God lovingly offered all of them a new beginning through Christ Jesus.

Once, during a men's retreat, I walked with a close friend toward our rooms at the end of a long day of prayer and study. This was a noble Christian, who, though retired, had spent his years praising the Lord with his life. He continued to care for those in need. But something at the retreat had convicted him deeply. He asked me why he had spent so many years of his life pursuing things that really didn't matter. I couldn't imagine a life more focused on the kingdom of God than his, yet somehow he felt he could have done more.

My first thought was to argue with him, telling him all the wonderful things he had done for the Lord. But I then realized God's word had deeply pierced his heart, so I instead offered him the thought that gets me out of bed every morning. In the kingdom of God, no matter where you are or where you've been, you can always begin again. It doesn't even take a new day. All it requires is a moment of quiet reflection, an intentional refocusing of your life, true repentance for where you've been, and then God graciously forgives and guides you to deeper life in his kingdom. God always wants a loving relationship with us.

This is one of the great joys of the Christian walk, the process of spiritual growth called sanctification. The Holy Spirit works in us to make us more and more like the God we love (2 Thessalonians 2:13). As we learn daily how to surrender our lives more completely to his guidance, we walk deeper into the heart of God's kingdom. One of the ways we make ourselves available to the Spirit of God for his sanctifying work is through the disciplines we will study in later chapters. But how do we begin the journey into the heart and love of God?

This question has caused great and numerous divisions among Christians. When is a person saved in Christ Jesus? How is a person saved in Christ Jesus? What must a person do to receive the gift of salvation? These are not unimportant questions, but the essential one is, "What do we mean by salvation?"

God's Loving Offer: Salvation!

For many, salvation is the final reward they will receive when they physically die. They believe that when they come to Jesus, they are forgiven of their sins, and then, if they remain faithful (defined in various ways) until their death, in the end they will be saved. Now, this view of salvation contains some truth, but it is only a partial view of God's gift of salvation. If we accept Jesus Christ as Lord and surrender our lives to him in obedience, we will live with him forever, a joy we will not fully experience until we die.

But what is the significance of our lives between conversion and death? Salvation is not just about a glorious future after death, but a present, living relationship. Salvation is living the life of Jesus, or perhaps better said, living life in Jesus. Jesus didn't come just to save us from our sins and receive us in heaven when we die; he came to save us from ourselves and save us for himself now!

The beginning of our spiritual journey is radically re-shaped if we view salvation as submitting our lives to the guidance of the Holy Spirit and becoming authentic disciples. If salvation is nothing more than placing my trust in God, so that when I die I will go to heaven, I can understand why there are different ideas about how this "salvation" occurs. Since (in this view) salvation is something that only God can see and that does not have real consequence in our daily lives, who's to know? When we reduce salvation to escape from hell or reward in heaven and forget it is all about relationship with God, then legalistic questions of salvation become all-important.

But salvation in Christ Jesus is so much more than that which happens when the physical body ceases to live. It is a new life —

now! Jesus said he came to bring life and to bring it in its fullness (John 10:10). This is how his disciples understood the life of Jesus. For example, John starts his first letter with a passionate plea for his readers to know Jesus Christ as he knew him, for all that John will teach grows out of his understanding of the life of his master:

> That which was from the beginning, which we have heard, which we have seen with our eyes, which we have looked at and our hands have touched—this we proclaim concerning the Word of life. The life appeared; we have seen it and testify to it, and we proclaim to you the eternal life, which was with the Father and has appeared to us. We proclaim to you what we have seen and heard, so that you also may have fellowship with us. And our fellowship is with the Father and with his Son, Jesus Christ. We write this to make our joy complete.   1 John 1:1-4

For John, Jesus was the embodiment of eternal life. John had seen it, touched it, and heard it. John himself was so full of life because of Jesus Christ that the only thing that could make his life better would be for those to whom he was writing to join him in fellowship with the Father and the Son. Don't miss the importance of his plea. Eternal life is not just for later. John wants you to find life and find it now. Jesus Christ is eternal life.

This life in Christ Jesus is so valuable that it makes all the world has to offer a disgusting pile of wet, smelly trash in comparison (Philippians 3:7-11). God offers this salvation life when we embrace his kingdom. Jesus claims he is the way, the truth, and the life. We enjoy access to the Father only through him (John 14:6). This is not a brash statement meant to condemn other religions; it is a clear statement of truth. We find life, in its fullest expression as God the creator intends it to be lived, only through Jesus. Jesus did not come to bring us a new religion; he came to bring us new life. Other religions may contain some truth. But

Jesus is the complete and full embodiment of truth. As such, he is the only way to salvation; he is the only complete and full expression of God (Heb. 1:3; Col. 2:9).

Breaking Away From Former Loves: Repentance

One does not casually walk into this distinctively different kind of life. We live life in God's kingdom with a different set of values than those espoused in this world. That is why both John the Baptist and Jesus came announcing repentance as the beginning step into kingdom life. There can be no new way until an old way has been tried and found wanting. The Good News from John and Jesus was that the kingdom of God was coming. There would be a time in the near future when humanity would be able to live within the end-time rule of God. But such a new life called for a drastic and dramatic change.

Have you ever been puzzled by John the Baptist's purpose? Why and how did he prepare the way of the Lord? He called people out of the cities, out of the relative comfort of their homes to repent of their present way of living and prepare themselves for the coming kingdom of God. It is interesting that John preached a baptism of repentance for the forgiveness of sins in anticipation of the coming kingdom (Luke 3:3). This confuses those who see the forgiveness of sins as salvation itself. The removal of sin is for walking in the kingdom. Forgiveness of sins is not an unseen heavenly reality that has little effect on the life of the forgiven. John's baptism prepared the way for the kingdom, at least for those who would accept his call.

The Pharisees and experts on the law were unable to understand God's purpose for their lives because they had refused John's baptism (Luke 7:29-30). They refused the preparation for the coming kingdom, which began with repentance. They rejected God's truth about themselves, "You are my beloved children," and preferred to try to earn the approval of God. Without understanding

God's gracious love, the message of Jesus made little sense to them. In that same passage, Jesus explains that when John came, lived an ascetic life, and called for repentance, they suggested John was crazy. When Jesus came demonstrating the joy of living in the kingdom of God, they called him a drunkard (Matthew 11:18-19). Their unrepentant hearts blinded them so they could not understand the cues of the kingdom. Without a willingness to repent, they had no hope for salvation life.

What constitutes repentance? It is not just saying that we are sorry for our sins. It is more than feeling bad about choices we have made. It is an admission of wrongful living. It is a willingness to experience a radical change of direction. It is turning away from one thing in order to embrace something new. One not willing to admit that his self-directed path is misguided cannot experience the joyful life of the kingdom.

When we come to the point in our lives where we realize that our self-directed steps lead only to weariness and continual failure, Jesus invites us to change direction and come to him. He will lovingly attach his life to ours "at the neck" (his yoke) (Matthew 11:28-29) so that we can learn from him how to live in the kingdom of God. The rest he offers is the experience of living in such a way that we know our lives are meaningful and purposeful. But we will never find that life apart from Jesus. There is no other way. He is "the way, the truth, and the life." We join Peter in his acknowledgment of what Jesus offers, "You have the words of eternal life. We believe and know that you are the Holy One of God" (John 6:68-69).

We can only follow Jesus by denying self and picking up our crosses (Matthew 16:24; Mark 8:34; Luke 9:23). The life to which Jesus invites us only comes through death to self. We cannot embrace the loving call of God until we are willing to let go of self-focused love. The call to self-death in the way in which Jesus taught it is a uniquely Christian idea. Unfortunately, many who claim to be Christians often ignore the call to die to self. But by refusing to embrace Jesus' call to death, we join the Pharisees in their inability to experience kingdom life. True life, salvation life in Jesus, comes after death of self. If we are unwilling to die, we will never find life. Jesus said, "For whoever wants to save his life will lose it, but whoever loses his life for me will save it. What good is it for a man to gain the whole world, and yet lose or forfeit his very self?" (Luke 9:24-25).

New Life, New Relationship, New Birth

Repentance leads to baptism, a ceremony of commitment to our new relationship with God. John the Baptist saw baptism as a sign of one's willingness to turn away from the fruitless life of self-worship in preparation for the realization of life in God's kingdom. He called his listeners to bear fruit demonstrating repentance. He told the tax collector to be honest and the soldier to live with integrity and contentment (Luke 3:7-14). While these may sound like simple, external changes, they are radical changes of heart and direction in life. We no longer live to expand our own kingdoms. We surrender our kingdoms to embrace an infinitely larger kingdom.

Jesus offered a baptism of ever-greater power. We who trust Jesus' redemptive work, who are willing to turn away from a life of self-direction, are cleansed of sin as we die to self in the grave represented by baptism. But that is not all! We are also ready to receive the Holy Spirit of God to live inside of us and direct our steps in the kingdom. Baptism is our invitation to participate in the drama of God's redemptive story. It is a sign of our willingness to take seriously the call to deny self, take up our cross, and follow Jesus. We hear the gospel. We realize the wrongful nature of our self-directed lives. With great remorse and growing excitement, we repent of that life away from God, we walk with our Lord into the grave, and we die.

The physical act of baptism in and of itself has no magical

power to save, just as a marriage ceremony has no force unless we take our vows seriously. Clearly where the New Testament mentions baptism, it intends submission of our lives to God in faith through Christ. Baptism is not a mindless ritual through which we magically receive salvation. It is an intentional walk into death, upon repentance, where we by faith encounter the blood of Jesus, which gives us new life. Baptism is not a physical bath, but a sign of an earnest appeal to God for a change of heart (1 Peter 3:21). Baptism is a participation in the death, burial, and resurrection of Jesus (Romans 6), preparing us for new life "walking with the Spirit" (Romans 8:1-8). Baptism is spiritual circumcision, initiating us into God's kingdom. There, one dead in sin comes alive through faith in the power of God to raise from the dead.

At a recent baptism, the idea of death came into clear focus. Broken-hearted about the life he had lived away from God, the man being baptized was now ready to embrace the kingdom and die to his former life. Just as I was ready to bury him in the water, he asked that we pray together. We did. He then asked me not to pull him out of the water until he squeezed my hand. He said simply, "There is a lot that I want to leave in the water. I am going to pray that God take all those things from my life. When I am ready for new life, I'll let you know." He waited so long that for a moment I was afraid he might be in danger of drowning. But he finally squeezed my hand. With joy, he embraced me. Full of new life and new identity, he was a new man. And indeed, he demonstrated a dramatically different life. He jokingly suggested we drain and change the water, because he left much of a former life at that moment of death.

Does baptism save us? Peter says it does (1 Peter 3:21). But remember our discussion of the nature of salvation. Relationship with God not only saves our life after death, it radically transforms daily life now. Repentance leads to a willingness to die, symbolized by baptism in water, in order that one might walk in newness of life. This action of baptism is not our work, but God's gracious invitation to participate in his redemptive narrative. As Paul told the Colossians, "In baptism you were buried with him and raised with him through your faith in the power of God, who raised him from the dead. When you were dead in your sins and in the uncircumcision of your sinful nature, God made you alive with Christ" (2:12, 13). With God graciously providing new life, the Holy Spirit then begins his sanctifying work in our lives, gradually transforming us as we learn daily to die to self.

What is this new life? Why is the Holy Spirit given? When one dies to self, life as it was once known comes to a dramatic end. Our old guidance system is destroyed. Our perspective of life is washed clean. What do we need most? God's Holy Spirit to enter into that new life as a new "guidance system." This new life is a life of trusting faith, where we diligently study the life of Jesus and yearn for the guidance of God's Spirit. A gradual transformation occurs as we mature in faith and learn more about God's intentions and purposes.

Several years ago, John Ortberg gave me a little card to put in my wallet. Since then, on a daily basis, it has been my first morning thought. It says, "My only reason to live is to live as Jesus would if he were in my place." At the bottom of the card Luke 6:40 is cited, "A disciple, when fully trained, will be like his master." A simple design of a stick figure leaving marks as he walks is at the bottom of the page. Another stick figure follows him, diligently attempting to place his feet in the imprints left by the one whom he follows.

I want my life to be more like that every day—beginning the day with the thought of dying to a self-directed life and intentionally placing my feet in the imprints left by Jesus. This is new life. At baptism I made my appeal to God for a changed heart, recognizing the emptiness of my life without him. Though I did not fully understand its meaning, I surrendered my will to his in the waters of baptism. I demonstrated my trust in God's power to cleanse me from my sin and raise me to new life. God then gave me his Spirit to convict me of my sins and change my heart into conformity with the heart of God.

This resurrection life occupies Paul's every waking thought. He has come to realize the surpassing value of knowing Christ Jesus, and all he wants in his life is to know Christ in an ever-increasing way. He forgets all that is behind him, all that he no longer values, and he presses on toward the fullness of Christ. This, he says, is the purpose of the cross (Philippians 3:7-21). Those who claim to be Christ-followers but continue to keep their minds on earthly things are actually enemies of the cross. For the cross transports us from the darkness of a living death to the light of kingdom life. We die to that meaningless life and are reborn in God's kingdom. How can we not continually fall deeper in love with a God who offers so much?

The Bride of Christ: God's Loving Purpose for the Church

What part does the church play in this drama? When we make our commitment to love God, we find ourselves in relationship with others who love him. The church is the fellowship of those who have died to self in order to embrace God's purposes for their lives. The church is not the focus of God's plan; it is the result of regenerated lives. It is the visible body of Christ in this world, as it takes seriously its call to be the assembly of the saved.

Jesus clearly identified what would demonstrate to the world the authentic nature of our discipleship. He said, "By this all men will know that you are my disciples, if you love one another" (John 13:35). We will come back to the church's role in spiritual formation in a later chapter. As we consider how God calls us to love him, we should remember that the church is primarily the community of those who have responded to the love of God, and who demonstrate that love by their love for one another and for all.

God has called us into fellowship with him. He created us to love him with all our heart, mind, and soul. This is where life is found. But to find it, we must turn away from self-worship and self-love, and learn to love God first. To that end, we run into the open arms of God's love, dying to self through the dramatic demonstration of death (baptism) and being reborn into the life he made us to enjoy—a life directed by the Holy Spirit and lived within the fellowship of his body, the church.

In God's love story for his people, perhaps the most beautiful picture of the church is provided in Revelation 19:7. Here, the church is the bride of the Lamb, wearing fine linen, bright and clean. The time is yet to come when our love for our Lord will be fully realized. And it will come. But that life in love with God begins with our commitment to him. In the chapters to come, we will look at ways to grow in that commitment.

For Personal Reflection

1. What do you remember about your initial response to God's loving call?

2. Have you truly repented of a self-focused life? What can help you do so?

3. In what ways does Jesus fully embody the perfect life? What does that perfect life look like? What is the relationship between his life and yours?

4. How do you seek the guidance of the Holy Spirit in your life?

Going Deeper

1. What do you need to do to stay focused throughout the day on God's love for you? Develop a plan to remind yourself—notes, reminders from friends, hourly thoughts, etc.

2. To what extent are you still drawn to the things of the world? What might you do to break your addiction to those things that ultimately have no meaning?

Group Work

1. Discuss your stories of "falling in love with God." When did you first commit to relationship with him? How did that feel? Do you have that same feeling today about your relationship?

2. Imagine ways you think the church can better reflect the love of God to the world. What specific things can we do to let people know they are loved by God?

3. Do you know someone who needs to make an initial commitment to God? List some ways we can encourage them to make that commitment. Share how we can help others hear the compelling call of God's love.

For Further Reading

For Beginners

Guiness, Os. *Rising to the Call: Discover the Ultimate Purpose of Your Life.* Nashville: W Publishing Group, 2003.

Reading Deeper

Hicks, John Mark and Taylor, Greg. *Down in the River to Pray: Revisioning Baptism as God's Transforming Work.* Siloam Springs, Arkansas: Leafwood Publishers, 2003.

Smith, Gordon T. *Beginning Well: Christian Conversion and Authentic Transformation.* Downers Grove: InterVarsity Press, 2001.

Spiritual Classics

Bonhoeffer, Dietrich. *The Cost of Discipleship.* New York: Simon and Schuster, 1995.

à Kempis, Thomas. *Imitation of Christ.* Nashville: Thomas Nelson, 1999.

Part 2

LIVING DAILY GOD'S LOVE

Human relationships are cultivated and
maintained by certain practices—listening,
communicating, sharing, and sacrifice. So, too,
there are regular practices that cultivate, maintain,
and embody our relationship with God.

CHAPTER FOUR

Listening to Our Beloved

When you first start dating someone, you hang on their every word. You want to know all about them. Where do they come from? What's their family like? What do they like to do? You listen closely not just to know about them, but to learn to know them intimately. Who are they really? What is in their heart?

It's the same way with our relationship with God. Having accepted his loving invitation to love, we want to know more about him. What's more, we want to listen to him with our heart, the very center of our being. We want to know the heart of God.

But we cannot make God talk. The good news is that he has not left us alone with no word from him. God has spoken! Where do we hear the voice of God? Primarily in Jesus, God's last and best word to his people, God's word made flesh (Hebrews 1:1-2; John 1:14). But where do we hear the voice of Jesus? Certainly, in Scripture, the word he breathes out to us (2 Timothy 3:16). We also hear him speak through his body, the church. In the company of others, loved by God and filled with his Spirit, we can discern his voice. We can learn to listen to the sometimes loud, sometimes gentle voice of God through Christ in all the events of life.

Listening to God can be a frightening experience, but it is more dangerous to live without hearing him. This is an invitation to hear the voice of God, the words of the one who loves us. To get to know him intimately through his word. Listen to what others around you are hearing. Be aware of his voice in the events of life. Come to this God of love with a humble heart to hear and to do the word of the Lord.

Hearing God in Scripture

We read in many ways. We might scan the newspaper for information, read a map for location, read a novel for pleasure, or read a textbook to pass a test. These are all good ways to read, depending on our circumstances.

A young soldier far away from home who receives a letter from his wife reads in yet another way. He might scan the letter quickly at first for news and information. But his longing for his beloved causes him to read the letter again and again, hearing her sweet voice in every line. He slowly treasures each word of this precious letter.

So also there are many good ways to read the Bible, depending on our circumstances. Bible study is absolutely necessary for our life with God. We rightly study the Bible for information. We ask, "Who wrote this?" "When was it written?" "Who were the original readers?" "How do these words apply to me?" More importantly, we want information about God. Who is he? What does he think of me? What does he want from me?

There is no substitute for this kind of close, dedicated Bible study. We must know what the Bible says to know our standing with God. We therefore read the Bible to discover true doctrine or teaching. But some, in their emphasis on the authority and inspiration of the Bible, have forgotten that Bible study is not an end in itself. We want to know God through Scripture. We want to have a relationship with the Teacher, not just the teachings.

Jesus tells some of God's people in his day, "You diligently study the Scriptures because you think that by them you possess eternal life. These are the Scriptures that testify about me, yet you refuse to come to me to have life" (John 5:39-40). He's not telling them to study their Bibles less, but he is reminding them of the deeper purpose of Bible study—to draw us to God through Jesus. Bible study is a means, not an end.

We read the Bible for more than information. By studying it, we experience transformation, the mysterious process of God at work in us. Through his loving words, God is calling us to life with him. He is forming us into the image of his Son.

Reading the Bible is not like reading other books. We are not simply trying to learn information or master material. Instead we want to stand under the authority of Scripture and let God master us. While we read the Bible, it reads us, opening the depths of our being to the overpowering love of God. "For the word of God is living and active. Sharper than any double-edged sword, it penetrates even to dividing soul and spirit, joints and marrow; it judges the thoughts and attitudes of the heart. Nothing in all creation is hidden from God's sight. Everything is uncovered and laid bare before the eyes of him to whom we must give account" (Hebrews 4:12-13).

One way of opening our hearts to the word of God is through meditation. Although this way of reading the Bible may be new to some, it has a long heritage among God's people. The Psalmist joyously meditates on the words of God (Psalm 1:2; 39:3; 119:15, 23, 27, 48, 78, 97, 99, 148). Meditation is taking the words of Scripture to heart and letting them ask questions of us. It is slowly chewing over a text, listening closely, reading God's message of love to us over and over. This is not a simple, easy, or naïve reading of Scripture, but a process that takes time, dedication, and practice on our part.

There are many ways to meditate on the Bible. One is praying the Scriptures. We will talk in the next chapter about ways to pray, but prayer and Bible study really cannot be separated. One way of praying the Bible is to make the words of a text your prayer. Obviously the prayer texts of Scripture, especially the Psalms, lend themselves to this. "The Lord is my shepherd" has been the prayer of many hearts.

However it is proper and helpful to turn the words of the Bible into prayers. Commands from God can become prayers. "You shall have no other gods before me" (Exodus 20:3) can be prayed, "Lord, keep me from anything that takes your place in my heart." Stories can be prayed. Jesus heals a man born blind (John 9), and so we pray, "Lord Jesus, open my eyes to who you truly are." Even the promises of the Bible become prayers. "Never will I leave you; never will I forsake you" (Deuteronomy 31:6; Hebrews 13:5) becomes "God help me know your promise that you are always with me and so live my life without fear."

One ancient way of meditation and praying the Scriptures is known as *lectio divina* or "holy reading." The first step along this way is listening to the Bible. Choose a biblical text that is not too long, perhaps seven to 12 verses. The purpose is to hear God's voice in your current situation, not to cover material or prepare lessons. Get into a comfortable position and maintain silence before God for several minutes. This prepares the heart to listen. Read slowly. Savor each word. Perhaps read out loud. Listen for a particular phrase that speaks to you. Ask God, "What are you trying to tell me today?"

The next step is to meditate on that particular phrase. That meditation may include slowly repeating the phrase that seems to be for you today. As you think deeply on it, you might even memorize it. Committing biblical passages to memory allows us to hold them in our hearts all day long. If you keep a journal, you might write the passage there. Let those words sink deeply into your heart.

Then pray those words back to God in your heart. Those words may call up visual images, smells, sounds, and feelings. Pay attention to what God is giving you in those words. Then respond in faith to what those words say to your heart. What do they call you to be and to do? Our humble response might take the form of praise, thanksgiving, joy, confession, or even cries of pain.

The final step in this "holy reading" is contemplation of God. We will talk more of contemplation in the next chapter on prayer. Again, one should not separate Bible reading from prayer. The words of God in Scripture transport us into the very presence of God where we joyfully rest in his love.

There are many helpful ways of hearing the voice of God in Scripture. Remember that the purpose of Bible reading and study is not to know more about the Bible, much less to pride ourselves as experts on Scripture. Instead, we read to hear the voice of our Beloved. We listen for a word of God for us.

Only Through the Bible?

Is the Bible the only way God speaks to us today? Many would insist that God speaks only through Scripture and that any-one who thinks otherwise really doesn't believe in the authority of Scripture. They believe that hearing God is simply a matter of intellectually studying the Bible and obeying what it says. However, those who seek to box God into the Bible actually detract from the authority of Scripture by trying to make it into something it is not. As we saw above in Jesus' warning, one can know the Scriptures but miss Jesus. Bible knowledge is not an end, but a means of hearing God.

To put it differently, what we desire and what God promises in the Bible is a personal relationship with him. But what kind of relationship can God have with his people if he hasn't spoken with them for two thousand years? The idea that God speaks only through the Bible and does not speak to us today is a form of bib-lical deism. It makes God into a once powerful deity that spoke and acted years ago, but since the ascension of Jesus has taken a long and silent vacation from the earth.

This view also denies the reality of the indwelling Spirit of God in our lives. Among other things, the Spirit pours God's love into our hearts (Romans 5:5), bears witness to our spirits that we are God's children (Romans 8:16), intercedes for us with God (Romans 8:26), and enlightens us as to God's will (Ephesians 1:17). Does all this happen merely by knowing the words of the Bible? No, the Spirit himself lives in us and guides us.

Let us be clear. We believe all Scripture is God-breathed (2 Timothy 3:16). It is the word of God written. As we saw in the section above, it is the primary way God speaks to us today. God is a consistent God who will never speak to us in ways contrary to the Bible (although he may very well speak in ways contrary to our understanding of the Bible). But our God is a living, active, loving God who seeks us in every aspect of life. He speaks through other people, through circumstances, and in the deep recesses of our hearts. Through his Spirit he enlightens us, not by inspiring new revelation so we can write new books of the Bible, but by opening our lives to what he is saying to us and to the churches through his word, the Bible.

Such an active, speaking God may be frightening to you. To say God speaks to us today does not mean that everyone who claims to hear God actually does. Both Old and New Testaments warn against false prophets, those who claim a word from God to gain power, money, and influence for themselves (see Isaiah 44:25; Jeremiah 14:14; 23:16; Lamentations 2:4; Ezekiel 13:9; 22:28; Matthew 7:15; 24:11; 1 John 4:1). Some who claim to speak from God have done much evil.

How then can we tell when God is speaking to us through others? It requires spiritual discernment, especially group discernment. We will say more about discernment in chapter six when we discuss Christian community. But briefly, one can tell false prophets by the way they live and what they think of Jesus (Matthew 7:16; 2 Peter 2:1-22; 1 John 4:1-2). Time will tell if they are sincere or if their works are a cloak for power and greed.

We should not be overly suspicious of those who say they have a word of God for us, immediately dismissing their advice, but neither should we be naïve about those who might deceive us. The key here is the golden rule. We trust others the way we want them to trust us. We trust until it is clear their actions and words mark them as deceivers, after their own interests, not ours or God's.

Hearing God through Others

The very fact that the Bible warns us to test prophets and spirits implies that God still speaks to us through others. Some will pass the test of discernment and have a word of God for us.

Think of all the people God has spoken through in your own life. For many of us, his first words for us came through our parents. Like Timothy, a loving grandmother and mother passed the faith on to us (2 Timothy 1:5). Not just in our childhood, but even now God speaks to us through the wise and caring words of our father and mother. He has spoken not only through their words, but by their examples. In them, we see what it means to call God Father and to experience him as a mother (Isaiah 66:12).

God speaks through other family members—husband, wife, brothers, sisters, children, aunts, uncles. Sometimes they give us a word of encouragement, sometimes advice, sometimes a warning. If we are listening, we can often hear God's voice in the faith of even the youngest children. How often do we take the time to listen closely to those who are closest to us? If we do listen, instead of taking our family for granted, we may find God speaking.

Friends are a wonderful gift from God. Everyone wants to have friends and to be a friend. Indeed, in our society we may suffer from "friend inflation," in that we have so many people we call friends that we have devalued friendship. When everyone is your friend, no one truly is.

But there are those we can call spiritual friends. Spiritual friendship is one that does not seek to have our needs fulfilled in friendship, but rather proclaims the reign of God over all. It is a dangerous love that opens us and our friends to the socially disruptive possibilities of the life of God. In other words, a spiritual friend cares more about our relationship to God than about our happiness or even about our friendship. Such friends can confront us in love about our weaknesses, gently restoring us to deeper fellowship in love (see Galatians 6:1-2). They can speak the tough words of God to us, words we would not hear if they came from those who did not love us.

God speaks through wise men and women who serve as spiritual mentors to us. We show wisdom if we seek the counsel of these wise ones. The book of Proverbs advises that we follow the path of the wise (Proverbs 8:33; 12:15; 15:31; 19:20; 22:17). One of the essential ways of growing spirituality is intentionally looking for those who can guide us spiritually with an attitude of humility.

There are times when God can even speak to us through strangers. We may meet those strangers in books we read. We might pass them on the street, in the supermarket, or in our neighborhood. Sometimes just a casual statement from someone we do not know can profoundly change our lives. That is God at work.

With all these voices clamoring for our attention—family, friends, mentors, strangers—how can we be sure they are speaking from God? Again the key is to listen. We must discern God's voice. We will come back to discernment in later chapters, but for now the task is to begin to listen to what God might be saying to us through others.

Hearing God through Nature

"The heavens declare the glory of God; the skies proclaim the work of his hands. Day after day they pour forth speech; night after night they display knowledge. There is no speech or language where their voice is not heard. Their voice goes out into all the earth, their words to the ends of the world" (Psalm 19:1-4).

Surely we have all heard the voice of God in nature. Perhaps in a glorious sunset placing multicolored streaks in the air amid thin swirling clouds, a scene more delicate and beautiful than any painting in any gallery in the world. Or in the riotous rebirth of spring with delicate flowers, budding trees, and greening grass. Or maybe in the awe of the roaring waves of the ocean at daybreak. Have you not heard his voice?

Truly hearing God's voice in nature depends on our appreciation of several biblical teachings. One is that God created nature. That means it is God's earth, not ours (Psalm 24:1-2), therefore we are not free to treat it any way we like. We must care for it as God's house, just as we use our best manners when visiting the house of a friend. God's creation of the earth also makes it impossible for us to worship the earth as a goddess, as some did in ancient times and a few do even today. Since the earth is God's creation, all things on earth are our fellow creatures. We were made from the dust of the earth (Genesis 2:7), but we have a special place in the creation, to care for it (Genesis 1:28; 2:15).

But the earth we live in is not the way God originally made it. As a result of the fall, weeds, thorns, pain, and death have entered our world (Genesis 3:16-20). To redeem his creation, God himself came to earth in the flesh (John 1:14). Jesus is redeeming the whole creation (Romans 8:4-9) and will return, bringing a new heaven and earth (2 Peter 3:10-13). The beautiful garden of paradise described in Genesis will be recreated through the power of the incarnation (Revelation 21:1; 22:1-5). The God who walked and talked with Adam and Eve in the garden will walk and talk with us.

But even now, as we anticipate that day, we need to be more attentive to the voice of God in the world around us. What is the content of this word from God? Is it merely a feeling of awe and wonder? Certainly our feelings are moved by the beauty and splendor of nature, but we also begin to know God in a new way as we experience his creation. We know he is a good God who gives rain and crops for food (Acts 14:17). We know he is a powerful God who made heaven, earth, and all that is in them (Romans 1:20). We stand amazed that this God beyond all imagination is the God who wants to know us and be our friend.

"Let the heavens rejoice, let the earth be glad; let them say among the nations, 'The Lord reigns!'" (1 Chronicles 16:31). And as they proclaim the reign of God, may we learn to listen.

Hearing God in All the Events of Life

God is at work in all the events of our lives, both good and bad (Romans 8:28), but it is often hard to see his hand at work. It is usually difficult to hear his voice.

Sometimes it seems easy, particularly when he answers prayer and showers blessings upon us. We pray to find a good man or woman who will be our companion for life in marriage. God answers that prayer beyond our imagination, giving us a partner and friend who constantly leads us closer to him. We pray for our children to be healthy, happy, and (most importantly) constantly trusting in a loving God. God gives us children of joy. We ask for spiritual friends to walk with us, for jobs that are callings to service, for a community of faith that surrounds us in love. God gives. We see his hand. We hear his voice in these acts saying, "You are my child whom I love."

But what about the tragedies of life, when it seems that God does not hear our cries? Is God silent? Has he turned his back on us? Both of the authors of this book lost their mothers at an early age. Did God make our mothers die? Did he refuse to answer our cries for their lives? Does God will everything that happens to us, even the bad?

Some think so. Their view of God's sovereignty is that every event comes directly from his hand. In an interview on television, the actor Robert De Niro was asked what God would say to him when he died. De Niro said he did not know, but "God would have a lot to answer for." Is God responsible for genocide, starvation, and the death of our loved ones?

No. Not every event in our lives comes directly from God. We live in a fallen, sinful world where God's good gift of free will has been turned against him and against others. God is a loving Father who only gives good gifts (James 1:17). Our God is so powerful that he can take the most evil events and bring good from them. There was nothing good about the deaths of our mothers. Death is evil, the last enemy of God to be destroyed (1 Corinthians 15:26). But looking back, it is clear that God was speaking to us in those horrible events, working not for our enjoyment at the time, but for our ultimate good. He used those evil events to bring us closer to him.

We may at first think it easier to hear God's voice when he showers blessings on us than when he works through the struggles of our lives. But he sometimes uses pain to get our attention. Perhaps even more difficult is to hear his voice on ordinary days. We most often hear God's voice in troublesome circumstances only in hindsight. That may tell us something about hearing the voice of God. We can only hear it when we take the time and have the perspective to listen. The busyness of life sometimes drowns out the voice of the Lord. We need to cultivate an awareness of God at work, to be silent enough to hear his voice. If we live more reflective lives, constantly asking ourselves, "What is God doing in my life today?" we are more likely to hear him.

Hearing the Gentle Inward Voice of God

Sometimes God does not shout at us through nature or through the circumstances of life, but instead gently whispers to us inwardly (1 Kings 19:12). As with all the other ways God speaks to us—through the Bible, others, nature, and life's events—there is danger in mishearing God's inward whisper. When we feel internal promptings they may come from our own desires, from Satan, or from God. We need to practice discernment to know whose voice is speaking.

But first we have to accept that God can and does speak this way to us. By "inward voice" we do not necessarily mean an audible voice. We have never heard an audible voice from God. Instead this is an inner prompting, sometimes in words, sometimes not. God may not always speak as dramatically to us as he did at times to Abraham, Moses, the prophets, and apostles, but his communication with us is no less real.

What we are talking about is a constant inward dialogue with God, a conversation where he sometimes gives us a clear word about what we should do. How do we know it is his word and not our own? We must test that voice by the Bible. God is consistent and will not speak contrary to his word in Scripture. We must bring that inward voice to the attention of others whom we trust, testing it by their spiritual insight. We must ask ourselves if what we think we hear is a selfish desire that ignores the needs of others or even does them harm.

However there are times when God tells us to do what we want to do. God wants us to enjoy him and be with him forever. Sometimes his desires go against our immediate wants, but sometimes his desires coincide with ours. God may be giving us exactly what we need, a word of encouragement or comfort. On the other hand, we can be fairly certain that the inward word we hear is from God if it calls us to service and sacrifice.

Listening to God

God is our loving Father who wants us to love him in return. He deeply desires a personal relationship with us. Father, Son, and Spirit make a home inside us (see John 14:16-17, 23). Our loving God speaks to his children! But we must listen for his voice. That listening is not a matter of gritting our teeth and trying harder to hear. Instead it is part of our entire life with God.

In the chapters to come we will talk about those regular practices that help us to hear. These include regular times for Bible study and prayer, silence, service, and worship. The primary way we listen to God is to walk with him each day. If we lovingly trust him and obey him in what we already know he wants, then he will reveal to us even more of his will. To genuinely hear we must act on what we have heard.

For Personal Reflection

1. How often do you study the Bible? Do you have a regular daily time of Bible study? Should you? How do you study the Bible? Are any of the ways of Bible study discussed in the chapter new to you? Which ones are you willing to try?

2. Does believing that God speaks in other ways in addition to speaking through the Bible detract from the authority of Scripture? What is the relationship between God speaking through the Bible and his other ways of speaking?

3. Briefly describe in writing (perhaps in your journal) a time when you heard the voice of God in nature. What was particularly striking about that experience? How did you feel at the time? How did that experience change your relationship to God?

4. Who has shaped your faith the most? Thank God for that person. Thank that person for passing on the faith to you. Who currently is your closest spiritual friend? What makes them so?

Going Deeper

1. Daily for one week, pray the words of a particular Bible passage, either as it is or turning it into a prayer. What insight did this give you into God?

2. Daily for one week take twenty minutes to meditate on Scripture using the method of *lectio divina* (see above pages for a description of the method). After a week, reflect on how this approach has shaped your encounter with God.

Group Work

1. Briefly describe a time in the last week that you felt God spoke to you through another person. Share those experiences with others in the group. Were there times in the last week when God spoke to someone else through you? If so, share those times.

2. Discuss what it means to be a spiritual friend. How does this differ from the usual meaning of friendship?

3. Have there been times recently when you heard the gentle, inward voice of God? Test those experiences with the group. What do the experiences of the group have in common? What does that say about how God speaks?

4. After a few moments of silence in the group, let each person reflect and then tell one way God has been at work in his or her life that day.

For Further Reading

For Beginners

Peace, Richard. *Contemplative Bible Reading: Experiencing God Through Scripture.* Colorado Springs: NavPress, 1998.

Reading Deeper

Blackaby, Henry and Richard. *Hearing God's Voice.* Nashville: Broadman & Holman, 2002.
Vest, Norvene. *Gathered in the Word: Praying the Scripture in Small Groups.* Nashville: Upper Room, 1996.
Willard, Dallas. *Hearing God.* Downers Grove, IL: InterVarsity Press, 1999.

Spiritual Classics

Guigo II, *The Ladder of Monks and Twelve Meditations.* Kalamazoo, MI: Cistercian Publications, 1979.

CHAPTER FIVE

Communicating with Our Beloved

In a loving relationship we not only listen to the one we love, but he listens to us. We are heard by God! The Almighty Ruler of the universe cares about our every desire, thought, and trouble. We listen and we are heard—this is communication and communion with God himself.

The word we use for this personal communication with God is prayer. Prayer is talking to and listening to God. But at its heart prayer is much more than that. It shapes the very relationship we have to the God who loves us, the God we love. Prayer is surrendering all that we are to the love and care of God.

Learning to Pray

We must learn to pray, because surrender of self does not come easy. But why learn to pray? We already know how! Practically everyone prays, even those who have little faith in God. We cannot remember a time when we did not pray. Perhaps you too have prayed all your life. So why do we need to learn how?

The disciples of Jesus also had prayed all their lives. From infancy their parents had taught them the way that the people of God should pray. Yet the disciples saw something in the prayer life of Jesus that caused them to ask, "Lord, teach us to pray" (Luke 11:1). Jesus had a deeper experience of prayer, a closer relationship to God than what these disciples had experienced. They wanted to share in that deeper experience.

That's what these chapters invite you to do, to enter a deeper experience of prayer. That doesn't mean that you have not prayed before or that you have not prayed "right." Prayer is not about getting a technique right. There are no shortcuts or tricks in our relationship with God. Prayer is about entering the very presence of God. We want to introduce you to many ways of praying; some of them may be new and strange to you. Give them a chance. However, we should always pray the way we can, not try to pray in ways we can't. Find the ways that are helpful to you, the ways that lead you to full surrender to God.

Praying Like Jesus

The authors of this book do not claim to be experts on prayer. Prayer is like the ocean. No one has completely fathomed the depths of the ocean (not even Jacques Cousteau), but even the smallest child can play in the waves by the shore. Like that child, we are still beginners in prayer, playing in the shallows.

But there is one who has plumbed the depths of prayer. His name is Jesus. He teaches disciples today to pray as he taught his disciples long ago. We are called to learn from him, not only what he taught about prayer, but how he himself prayed.

Jesus, the eternal Son of God, the Word made flesh, felt the need to pray. Have you ever thought how profound that is? Jesus prayed. That might give us both a deeper view of Jesus and of prayer. We used to think that Jesus had a direct pipeline to God, that he automatically knew and followed the will of God at every moment. But Jesus was human. He struggled with doubts and fears. If Jesus the eternal son of God felt the need to be with his Father in prayer, how much more do we?

Jesus had a regular practice of making time to be alone with God. Do you? Do you have a set time and place for daily prayer? If not, what is our excuse? Too busy? Not enough time?

Are we busier than Jesus? Mark 1:21-39 tells us of a long day in the life of Jesus. In the morning he preaches in the synagogue in Capernaum. People are amazed at his authoritative teaching and more amazed when he casts a demon out of a man in the synagogue. He then goes to Simon Peter's house and heals Simon's mother-in-law from a life-threatening fever. The whole town hears about it, and after dark they bring all their sick to be healed by Jesus.

What does Jesus do after a long day of work? Does he take the next day off? No. "Very early in the morning, while it was still dark, Jesus got up, left the house and went off to a solitary place, where he prayed" (Mark 1:35). Can you not find time to be alone with God? Here's a radical suggestion: set the alarm clock thirty minutes early. That's what Jesus did. Why? Because he felt the need to be alone with the God who loves him. But Jesus is so busy, the disciples won't leave him alone. They find him and wonder why he left such a successful ministry in Capernaum. "Everyone is looking for you!" they say. But Jesus has received strength and direction for his life. God gave them to him in prayer.

Another busy day. Jesus hears that John the Baptist has been killed. He tries to be alone with God in that time of crisis, but people hear where he is going and a huge crowd follows him. He has compassion on them because they are like sheep without a shepherd. He feeds them with the word of God. He feeds them miraculously with a few loaves and fish. Then he does a most amazing thing. He sends the disciples away and dismisses the crowd. Why? What can be more urgent than telling the good news to those ready to hear?

Being alone with God is more urgent. "Immediately Jesus made the disciples get into the boat and go on ahead of him to the other side, while he dismissed the crowd. After he had dismissed them, he went up on a mountainside by himself to pray. When evening came, he was there alone" (Matthew 14:22-23). Perhaps, like Jesus, we must wait until late at night when the long day of work is over, when the kids are in bed and everything is silent, to make time to be alone with God in prayer.

Sometimes early. Sometimes late. "But Jesus often withdrew to lonely places and prayed" (Luke 5:16). Jesus cultivated a habit of prayer to God. He made the time because he knew that nothing was more important, nothing more essential. If Jesus needed to be alone with God, how much more do we?

What keeps us from it? It's hard! It is very difficult to be consistent in our prayer time. The spiritual exercise of prayer is similar to physical exercise. For years I knew I should exercise for my health, so I exercised when I felt like it—which meant I did not exercise much. To get the benefit from physical exercise, one must do it regularly. For me, that means I do pretty much the same exercise at the same time every day, even when I don't especially feel like it.

It's the same way with prayer. If I fail to plan to pray, I fail to pray. If we are to pray like Jesus, then we must often, regularly, daily withdraw to be alone with God. Even on days when we don't feel like praying or we don't enjoy prayer, we still cultivate the habit, the regular practice of prayer.

To pray like Jesus means to have a regular period of prayer. It also means we pray to God in times of crisis. Jesus prayed all night before choosing the twelve apostles (Luke 16:12-16). He did not rely on his own wisdom in making this decision, but on the will of his Father. Jesus was praying when he revealed himself as the Messiah to those apostles (Luke 9:18-22). While he was praying, he was transfigured before Peter, James, and John, shining with the glory of God (Luke 9:29-36). In the same way we see Jesus more clearly when we pray.

In the greatest crisis of his life, Jesus prayed. Facing the cross, he prayed with tears, cries, and bloody sweat, "My Father, if it is possible, may this cup be taken from me. Yet not as I will, but as you will" (Matthew 26:39). He prayed from the cross, "My God, My God, why have you forsaken me?" (Matthew 27:45-46). "Father, forgive them, for they do not know what they are doing" (Luke 23:34). "Father, into your hands I commit my spirit" (Luke 23:46).

This last prayer from the cross expresses the whole of the prayer life of Jesus. He is not simply sending his spirit to God in hope of the resurrection. At every fork in the road of his life, with every breath including his last Jesus committed himself to God. Prayer is surrender to the will of the Father. It is trusting all that we are to him.

What does it mean to pray like Jesus? It means we make regular times to be alone with God. It means we can turn to God in crisis, because we have developed a relationship to him in those regular times of prayer. Most of all, it means we surrender all that we are (this is what Jesus means by his "spirit") to the hands of a loving Father.

Praying With Jesus

But who can perfectly follow the example of Jesus? Who can pray like him? He is Jesus. We are not. How can we on our own strength pray the way he prayed? Must we ask, "What would Jesus do?" and then go do it?

The relationship between Jesus and us in prayer is much more dynamic than merely following his example. We not only pray like Jesus, we pray with him. Or better, he prays with us. This is what we mean when we end our prayers "In Jesus' name." It means Jesus lives inside us and is struggling with us in prayer. As Paul said, "to live is Christ" (Philippians 1:21) and "I no longer live, but Christ lives in me" (Galatians 2:20). Christ lives to intercede for us (Hebrews 7:25). He is always right there praying with us.

The Spirit also prays in us. "In the same way, the Spirit helps us in our weakness. We do not know what we ought to pray for, but the Spirit himself intercedes for us with groans that words cannot express" (Romans 8:26). Before his death, Jesus tells the disciples he must leave them, but he will not leave them orphaned, he will come to them (John 14:18). He promises to come and live with his people through his Spirit (John 16:7).

Jesus, the Spirit, and the Father himself live in us. "Jesus replied, 'If anyone loves me, he will obey my teaching. My Father will love him, and we will come to him and make our home with him'" (John 14:23). When we pray, we never pray alone. It is not only our hearts that we bring before God. God himself is with us—Father, Son, and Spirit. He prays in us.

Do we need the discipline to pray regularly as Jesus did? God works within us to give us that discipline. Do we need power from God in time of crisis? His power lives in us. Do we need faith to surrender all we are to God? God gives us the strength to let go and commit ourselves to him.

But exactly how did Jesus pray? How does he pray through us? We are not told in the Bible exactly how Jesus prayed. He gives instruction on prayer. He even gives the Lord's Prayer as a model. But we do not have a detailed account of how Jesus prayed. Why not? Because God intends the relationship between Jesus and us in prayer to be living and active. If God had given us a single model of prayer, it would easily become routine and rote. We might easily think that prayer was about getting the words right instead of being about a relationship with a loving, active God.

In other words, by saying we pray like Jesus and that he prays with us, we are not saying that we all must pray exactly the same. We give examples below of ways to pray. None is the only right way. Any may be right for you, provided your intention is for a closer relationship with God. The important thing is to be willing to learn to pray.

In the words of Thomas Merton in *Contemplative Prayer,*

One cannot begin to face the real difficulties of the life of prayer and meditation unless one is perfectly content to be a beginner and really experience himself as one who knows little or nothing and has a desperate need to learn the bare rudiments.

As beginners, here are some ways to pray. As you try them, remember it is Jesus who is teaching us to pray and who is praying alongside us.

Saying our Prayers

One of the ways many of us first learned to pray was by praying rote, memorized prayers—"Now I lay me down to sleep..." or "God is great, God is good, let us thank him for our food." In church we learned other set prayers, particularly the Lord's Prayer.

Perhaps because we learned these in childhood, we think that saying our prayers is a form of prayer we have outgrown. But many Christians throughout the ages and today find it helpful to have set prayers they read as part of their daily time with God. In the last chapter, we suggested praying Scripture, especially the Psalms. These written prayers soon become our own words, not just the words of Scripture or of earlier believers.

There is a danger in saying our prayers. Even saying the Lord's Prayer several times daily can become an empty ritual (Jesus warned against empty words in prayer in Matthew 6:7), but it need not become that. We can mean words we say each day. Each day I leave my wife with the words, "I love you." No doubt I sometimes feel the meaning of those words more deeply than at other times. But I always mean them.

In the same way, repeated, familiar prayers can be heartfelt and can train our hearts in prayer to God. Perhaps we sometimes confuse spontaneity with spirituality. To be thoughtful in prayer, in the words we say to God, is always a good thing. At the end of this chapter, we suggest some daily prayer books that can be used to guide our thoughts and focus our intentions when we pray.

Speaking with God

Prayers written by others can become our prayers, but if all we do is say others' prayers, we miss out on a great blessing. We are also privileged to come to God with our own words. Paul gives us four descriptions of the types of words we use in prayer: "I urge, then, first of all, that requests, prayers, intercession, and thanksgiving be made for everyone" (1 Timothy 2:1). To these, other passages add confession (1 John 1:9) and lament (Psalm 102:1). "Prayers" is a general term, perhaps referring to those memorized or written prayers discussed above.

When we speak to God, we make **requests**. This is the popular view of prayer in our culture. For some, it is their whole view of prayer. On the old Flip Wilson television show, Flip would announce, "I'm about to pray; do you want something?" We can misunderstand prayer and limit God to an eternal shopkeeper ready to provide whatever we ask.

But it is always right to take our requests to God. Why? Because he is a loving Father who wants to care for his children. That doesn't mean he always gives us what we ask for, just as we who are loving parents don't give our kids everything they want. Why not? Because they don't always know what's best for them. Because we want to teach them what they truly need.

No request is too small or too great to take to God. The Bible is full of people asking God for a variety of needs—healing, guidance, protection, children, food, comfort—the list is nearly endless. We should never hesitate to take our needs and our desires to God.

But how do we know when he answers? If our requests are met, that is a clear answer. But what if we do not get what we ask for? What if we can't seem to get an answer from God?

God answers all prayers, but we need to discern, to listen for his answer. Sometimes we must wait long and hard for the answer. Sometimes we must wrestle with the will of God for us. We will discuss this process of discernment below in chapter seven. For now, let us boldly bring our requests to God and trust that he is a loving Father who hears us. He may not answer how or when we want, but he intimately cares for all our concerns.

Along with prayers and requests we also give thanks to God when we pray. **Thanksgiving** is closely related to praise. In the words of Meister Eckhart, "If the only prayer you say in your whole life is 'Thank you,' that would suffice." While something of an overstatement, this is a reminder that gratitude is the basic stance of a child of God.

In prayer, we praise God for all he is and all he has done for us. We come not only with requests but with thanksgiving for how God has blessed us in the past. It might even help to keep a gratitude journal, listing all the ways God has blessed us each day. Gratitude keeps our hearts open before God, ready to receive what he thinks is best for us. Our entire lives in Christ are "thank-you lives," with every day a response to God's wonderful gifts.

In prayer we freely confess our sins before God. We not only bring to mind specific sins, but we admit that we are sinful, broken, fallen creatures. Sin means falling short of what God intended us to be. He created us for fellowship with him, to love him and enjoy his love forever. But we all have broken relationship to God, preferring our ways to his. This we confess in prayer.

However, our focus in **confession** is not on our specific sins or overall sinfulness, but on the forgiveness of God. If, "God, have mercy on me, a sinner" (Luke 18:13) is the content of every prayer we pray, "Then neither do I condemn you" (John 8:11) is the answer to every confession. Simply feeling bad about our sin helps no one. Instead, we turn from our sinfulness and turn to the God who forgives, restores, and empowers us with his Holy Spirit.

At times we come to God burdened not only by our sins, but

by terrible circumstances. We pour out the pain of our hearts in **lament.** Prayer, like life itself, is not always an enjoyable experience. In all the ways of praying we will discuss, we must remember that prayer is about relationship with God. As in all relationships, even our most joyous ones, there are times of pain and strain. God is our loving Father, but we do not always like what he does or understand when it seems he is doing nothing to help us. In those times of trial, we can be honest with God in prayer. We do not have to pretend before God. He knows our hearts, even when they are breaking. God's people have always felt the freedom to complain to God. Look at the prayers of Job, the Psalmist, or the writer of Lamentations (imagine a whole book of the Bible with this title!). Even Jesus, the beloved Son of God, laments. From the cross he cries, *"Eli, Eli, lema sabachthani?"* that is, "My God, my God, why have you forsaken me?" (Matthew 27:46).

What kind of faithful prayer is this? This is a cry of pain. The pain is so intense, the scene so memorable, that Matthew records the very words Jesus spoke in Aramaic. In the past at times of crisis, the Father had appeared in a cloud to proclaim Jesus as his "beloved Son." Now on the cross there is nothing but silence from the Father. At times we have all felt abandoned by God; we all have cried in pain. Jesus was truly abandoned by God.

Yet this cry is also a cry of hope. Hope? Yes, for Jesus here is not using his own words, but is quoting the first line of Psalm 22. Jesus knew his Bible, and we can be sure he quoted this verse with the entire Psalm in mind. In Psalm 22, David cries to the Lord in pain, but (as in many of the Psalms) this cry of pain ends in a confession of faith and hope in God. Though the Psalmist feels forsaken, in truth he knows the Lord "... did not despise or abhor the affliction of the afflicted; he did not hide his face from me, but heard me when I cried to him" (Psalm 22:24).

Jesus' cry sounds like a cry of hopelessness, but although he quotes only the first verse, he knows this Psalm ends in hope. Abandoned by his Father, Jesus knew that ultimately God would hear his cry and deliver him. And God did by raising him from the dead.

If we are to pray like Jesus and (what is more) have Jesus pray in us, we must learn to lament. We dare not try to hide our feelings from our Father. Instead we share our deepest pain in trust that God will hear and will act on our behalf.

Listening in Prayer

Prayer is more than talking to God; it also means listening to him. In chapter four, we looked at different ways of listening to God. We also hear his voice in prayer. We hear him when he answers our requests, when he accepts our praise and thanksgiving, when he hears our confession and forgives us, and when he shares the pain of our laments. Hearing God in prayer requires the discernment we will discuss below.

However, one way we speak to and hear God in prayer is **intercession**. We sometimes use intercession to mean requests we make for others. It is always right to bring specific requests for other people to God. Many ask us to pray for them in crises of health, loss, and despair. It is our privilege to pray for them.

But what happens when you don't know how to pray for someone? At times we do not know what is best for them or what God wants for them. In those times, we intercede with God for them. The prayer of intercession (as contrasted with requests for others) consists of asking, "What is God's prayer for this person?" In other words, we are lifting up this person in prayer to God, asking him to bless and guide as only he knows how.

This requires that we quietly listen to what God tells us for this person. It requires asking if there is something in us that might have to change for us to pray God's prayer for this person. Intercession is thus dialogue with God on behalf of another. We place someone on our heart and bring that heart to God in humility, not asking that God will do what is best for us, but what is best for that someone.

Praying with Our Bodies

We pray to God, and he prays in us, through our bodies. God loved us enough to form our bodies from the dust of the earth (Genesis 2:7). Our bodies are temples of the Holy Spirit and we are to glorify God in our bodies (1 Corinthians 6:13-20). Christian spirituality is embodied spirituality. We pray not only with mind, soul, or heart, but with our whole selves, including our bodies.

Thus it is important to discuss prayer postures. There is, of course, no right or perfect prayer posture, as if getting in a certain body position will automatically make us spiritual. Prayer is about relationship with God, and there are no tricks or shortcuts in relationships. However, it may be that our prayer life is impoverished by placing too little emphasis on how we pray with our bodies. If we are to learn to pray from God in Scripture and from Jesus himself, we should look at how people of faith prayed with their bodies.

The typical position for approaching the almighty God is stretched out **face down**. Abraham (Genesis 17:3, 17), Moses and Aaron (Numbers 16:22; 20:6), Joshua (Joshua 7:6), Jehoshaphat (2 Chronicles 20:18), and Ezekiel (Ezekiel 1:28) all fall on their faces in the presence of the Holy God. Peter, James, and John do the same when they hear the voice of God (Matthew 17:6). Around the throne of God in heaven, the angels and elders fall down and worship (Revelation 7:11).

Do you ever pray facedown before the Lord? This is a posture best used at home in our private times with God. What are we saying with our bodies when we fall down before the Lord? That he is God and we are not. That we are in the very presence of the Almighty and the All-Holy. We say, "God, be merciful to me a sinner!" This is the posture of humility and awe.

God's people also **bow** before him (Genesis 24:26, 48, 52; Exodus 34:8; 1 Chronicles 29:20). The Magi bow before baby Jesus

(Matthew 2:11). Bowing may mean falling facedown, bowing from the waist, or bowing the head. In this position we also are expressing with our bodies the awe, respect, and worship we have for God.

Through the ages God's people have **knelt** in prayer (1 Kings 8:54; Matthew 20:20; Ephesians 3:14). This is the posture of a servant, acknowledging that Jesus is our Lord. The day is coming when every knee shall be bent in homage to God and Christ (Romans 14:11; Philippians 2:10).

The favorite prayer posture of Jesus himself is **standing**, looking upward (Matthew 14:19; Mark 7:34; John 11:41), although in Gethsemane he fell with his face to the ground (Matthew 26:39). Standing, looking upward into heaven expresses our desire to see God face to face. He is the Almighty God, but he is also the God of love who wants relationship with us. When we talk to our loved ones, we look them in the eye. So praying looking up is our way of staring into the face of the God we love.

Perhaps while standing, Jesus, like others, **lifted his hands** in prayer (Nehemiah 8:6; Psalm 28:2; 1 Timothy 2:8). We lift our hands to praise God and to receive his blessings.

Have you tried these postures in prayer? Why not? We need to learn to pray with our entire selves including our bodies. These postures express what is on our hearts. They also can change our hearts. It's hard to be proud with your face to the ground! We always express our affections bodily with smiles, frowns, hugs, and handshakes. Let us be free to express with our bodies our love for the one who first loved us.

Some even combine many of these postures and others into "body prayers." For example, begin by standing with your feet slightly apart. Then gently reach down, touch the floor and say, "I praise you God for the earth you have made." Slowly stand, reach out your arms as wide as you can and say, "I embrace the world with your love." Hold that postion for a moment, then stretch your hands open above your head and say, "I give all glory to you, my God."

In the next chapter, we will look at other ways we relate to God in prayer, particularly listening in silence. For now let us intentionally and thoughtfully practice those forms of prayer that may be familiar to us—prayers, requests, thanksgiving, confession, lament, and intercession. Let us pray with our bodies, perhaps in ways unfamiliar to us. By praying in these ways, let us remember that Father, Son, and Spirit pray in us and with us.

For Personal Reflection

1. Do you have a time set aside each day for prayer? If so, how has that time alone with God helped you? If not, what has kept you from making time to be alone with God?

2. Which type of prayer in this chapter do you pray most often? Which do you pray least often? What does that tell you about your relationship to God?

Going Deeper

1. Take 15 minutes each day for a week and pray from a book of prayer (see suggestions in the bibliography). At the end of the week reflect on whether those words have become your own in prayer.

2. Write a letter from God to you. What would God say to you concerning your life the past week?

3. Each day this week in your prayer time alone with God, pray with a different posture. At the end of the week reflect. How do different postures affect the quality of your praying?

Group Work

1. Discuss with the group your reaction to the different ways to pray discussed in this chapter. Which way do you find most comfortable? Which way is newest to you? Are you willing to try "new" ways to pray? Why or why not?

2. Do we need to learn to pray "right"? How can we learn to do so? Can concern for praying "right" get in the way of prayer? How?

3. Discuss what you want most from God at the present time. Have you asked him for it? Has he answered?

4. Let each person in the group share a need. What is your initial reaction to these needs-to help them or to pray? Which is more important?

For Further Reading

For Beginners

Paulsell, William O. *Rules for Prayer.* New York: Paulist Press, 1993.

Reading Deeper

Houston, James. *The Transforming Power of Prayer.* Colorado
    Springs: NavPress, 1996.
Vennard, Jane. *Praying with Body and Soul: A Way to Intimacy with
    God.* Minneapolis: Augsburg, 1998.
Wolpert, Daniel. *Creating a Life with God: The Call of Ancient Prayer
    Practices.* Nashville: Upper Room Books, 2003.

Daily Prayer Books

Shorter Christian Prayer. New York: Catholic Book Publishing, 1988.
Webber, Robert. *The Book of Daily Prayer.* Grand Rapids: Eerdmans,
    1993.
Webber, Robert. *The Prymer: The Prayer Book of the Medieval Era
    Adapted for Contemporary Use.* Brewster, Massachusetts:
    Paraclete Press, 2000.

Spiritual Classics

Allen, Leonard. *The Contemporaries Meet the Classics on Prayer.* West
    Monroe, LA: Howard Publishing, 2003.

CHAPTER SIX

Being with Our Beloved

If you love someone, you want to talk with them and listen to them. However, if you are comfortable in your relationship, there are times when you can be together and say nothing to each other. You just enjoy each others company and want to waste time and do nothing together.

It's the same way in our relationship with God. We don't have to be always saying things to God in prayer. Many times it is enough to be with him. That comfortable companionship with him can be even richer than our experiences of spoken prayer.

The Need for Silence

There are many forms of silence. First-date silence is awkward and embarrassing. All the while, you're trying to think of what to say, worried that you might look like a fool. You might even memorize certain lines or practice certain conversational topics-"My, don't you look nice tonight" or "What is your favorite movie?"— to decrease that awkwardness. So also as we begin to pray, we may feel clumsy, relying on rote prayers and set forms to know what to say to God.

As you get to know your date better, you begin to fall in love and feel more at ease. This is the stage where you bare your heart, pouring out your inner feelings in a rush of words. This is the stage where you listen long and hard to this fascinating person who loves you and accepts you as you are. In our relationship with a loving God, these are the times when words come easily and we long to listen to his word. The prayer practices discussed in the last chapter come to the fore in this stage.

However, after more than twenty-five years of marriage I find I can sit long hours with my wife, saying little or nothing. This is not awkward silence as with a first date. This is not the silence of anger after an argument. This is a fully trusting silence where we know each other so well we don't need to say a thing. This is a loving silence that finds joy, contentment, and communion in simply being with the other.

That's the kind of silence we can have with God—being with him, resting in his presence, feeling his gentle touch upon us. Such silence is called for in Scripture: "Be still, and know that I am God" (Psalm 46:10). The prophets say that those who worship idols must shout to try to wake them up (since they are lifeless). "But the Lord is in his holy temple; let all the earth be silent before him" (Habakkuk 2:20). We do not have to convince God to care for us with shouts and many words (see Matthew 6:7-8). All we need to do is be with him in silence. He is in his holy temple, not far removed from us, but in our bodies and in our churches—these are the temples of God (1 Corinthians 3:16; 6:19).

When Jesus spent time alone with God, we believe at least part of that time must have been spent in silence. Before Jesus chooses the twelve apostles, he spends the night in prayer (Luke 6:12). Have you ever tried to pray all night? A few years ago, if I had tried it would have gone something like this. I would have praised God for who he was, thanked him for all my blessings, confessed my sins, and brought my requests to him for others and myself. Then I would have looked at my watch and thought, "Wow, seven more hours to go."

So what did Jesus do all night in prayer? We are not told. We can imagine that he prayed in all the ways listed above and that he brought the names of prospective apostles before his Father. However, we've got to believe that he spent a great deal of that time in silence, resting in the presence of God.

But for us silence is difficult. Why? For several reasons. We are too busy, and we think being silent and doing nothing is a waste of time. Yet as we saw in the previous chapter, this is exactly what Jesus did. In the middle of a busy ministry, he made time to be alone and "waste time" with God.

We also must be willing to "waste time" with God. Being silent with him for fifteen minutes to an hour daily is a way of acknowledging that he is God and we are not. He can run the world without us. It is a way of admitting that we rely on the power of God, not on our own brilliance, planning, and efforts. It is a confession that God is an active God, who works in prayer. Thus we are not being lazy and unproductive by "wasting time" with God, but we are putting ourselves in the place where he can work through us.

Silence is also painful to us because when we are alone with God we are also alone with ourselves. We sometimes make ourselves busy merely to avoid self-reflection. Even if you keep a clean house, the bright sun shining through a window can reveal all kinds of dust. Likewise, in the light of the glory and goodness of God, our own faults are revealed. We see ourselves as we really are: sinful, broken, proud, self-deceived. But in the pain of that self-revelation there is also joy. God loves us as we are. Christ and the Spirit are at work in us, making us clean in God's sight. The cleansing power of solitude is both painful and joyous.

Perhaps the greatest difficulty of silence is that it calls for full surrender to God. It is frightening to honestly open our hearts to others, even to God. In this silence God may call us to a life we are trying to avoid. A life we do not control. A life of suffering. A life of service. If we spend time with him, God will call us to make changes, specific changes we may want to avoid. Silence calls us to receive from God, to let go, to let him shape and mold us. Surrender is not easy.

Thus solitude is not a way of escaping from the responsibilities of life or avoiding difficult people. However, like Jesus, we must find the time and the place to be alone with God so we can receive from him the strength to love others. The greatest gift we can give to those we love is to separate ourselves from them for a while each day so we can be with the source of our love.

Silence and solitude do not take the place of other forms of prayer. With those we love there are times of comfortable silence, but also times for speaking and listening. Silence is not necessarily a higher form of prayer, but simply another way we can enjoy our relationship to God.

Contemplative Prayer

Silence. Solitude. Surrender. Perhaps you are ready to try this way of being with God, but you don't know where to start. One way of being silent before God is called **contemplative prayer**. There are many types of contemplation, but what they all have in common is intentionally experiencing a silent longing for God, a deep, inward look at the One who is all.

One form of contemplation is **centering prayer**. One begins by sitting in a relaxed position, feet on the floor, usually with eyes closed. Become aware of your breathing. Remember your intention to be in the presence of God. As a reminder of that intention, choose a prayer word (Jesus, Father, Spirit, peace, presence, rest, or another) and gently introduce that word into your silence. When you become aware of anything that distracts you, whether outward noises or inward thoughts, softly return to your prayer word to remind you of your intent to be with the Lord.

The prayer word is not meant to be a mantra that is repeated continually, but instead is a way of refocusing our whole being on God. In a twenty-minute period of centering prayer, you might be distracted and have to return to your prayer word dozens of times. That's fine. God honors every intent to come to him. For some people, a visual image helps in this regard. Some visualize a great warming light that so fills them that distractions are lost in its glow. Others picture themselves immersed in the love of God, with thoughts floating overhead on the surface of the water. One cannot help having thoughts in contemplative prayer. The idea is not to fight the thoughts but to let them go, flowing down the stream of consciousness.

Again, try this method, but keep what works for you. This and other contemplative methods are not shortcuts, but merely tools. The goal is to rest in God, not to fight our way to him. If you have trouble sitting silently with God (and everyone does at times), do not give up but do not try harder. Just try consistently. Let go and allow him to fill you and pray wordlessly in you.

Contemplative prayer is an act of pure faith. We trust that God is with us and works in us even when we do not feel him at work. You may be exalted in joy in contemplation. You may be filled with despair and pain. Most of the time you may feel nothing and wonder if this prayer is "working." Keep trusting that God is at work, no matter what you feel. It is God we want, not exalted feelings.

The Constant Presence of God

How do we take the experience of God we find in contemplation and live it throughout the day? There are many ways to pray that serve as constant reminders of God in us. These do not create God's presence (he is always with us), but they focus our attention on that presence.

Earlier we spoke of hearing the voice of God in **nature**. One way to be in constant prayer is to be aware of the beauty of creation. In the words of William Blake, "To see the world in a grain of sand, and heaven in a wild flower." Distracted by the busyness of contemporary life, it takes great effort on our part to stop and view a sunset, enjoy the smell of new-mown grass, listen to the song of a bird, or lightly touch the petals of a rose. Yet in these simple acts we remind ourselves of the God who made us, sustains us, and beautifies us. All beauty comes from God.

We can also hear the voice of God and experience his presence in **all the events of life**. When people interrupt us and become inconvenient, we can see the face of God in those made in his image. When the "idiot" cuts us off in traffic, we can pray for him or her, knowing that God is Father of all. With every small ache or sharp pain, we can praise the God who shares our agony and heals our lives. When hungry, we remember the One we truly hunger for. When eating, we give thanks to God who gives daily bread. Every event can be a reminder of his presence.

Not just every event that happens to us, but **every action of the day** can also be a prayer. "And whatever you do, whether in word or deed, do it all in the name of the Lord Jesus, giving thanks to God the Father through him" (Colossians 3:17). Tasks that may seem insignificant—brushing teeth, making beds, washing dishes—can all be done in gratitude to God, reminding us of his work in us.

Specific times of prayer can recall our attention to God. Of course we will have our extended prayer times to be alone with God, but here we mean brief words of prayer throughout the day. Some pray on the hour. If you have a watch or clock that chimes each hour, it can serve as a reminder to briefly bow, give thanks to God, and be aware of his presence. The early church had times for prayer (Acts 3:1), and it would help us to have them.

Practicing the Presence

There are other specific ways of praying that constantly focus us on God. One is **breath prayer**. Since we are always breathing, in this act we can be conscious of the gift of life and the Giver of life. In the beginning, God breathed life into us (Genesis 2:7). After his resurrection, Jesus gave the Holy Spirit to his disciples by breathing on them (John 20:22). Indeed, in the original languages of the Bible, "spirit" (whether our human spirits or the Holy Spirit) and "breath" are the same word.

How can breathing be a prayer? By attention and intention, like every kind of prayer. Begin by paying attention to your breathing. Breathe deeply and regularly from the diaphragm, noticing how you breathe. As you take in air, think of God filling you with the breath of life. As you breathe out, think of God's Spirit living in you and being breathed from you to others in love.

In this simple act of breathing, we acknowledge our dependence on God and his powerful work within us. After a few moments of breath prayer, we may feel ready for a longer period of contemplative prayer. At other times, a short period of breath prayer can calm us and focus us in the middle of distractions and crisis. We breathe all the time. We can make every breath a prayer.

Another form of constant communion with God is the **Jesus prayer**. It is a continual cry for help, based on the story of blind Bartimaeus who hears Jesus coming and shouts repeatedly, "Jesus, Son of David, have mercy on me!" Jesus hears, calls Bartimaeus, and heals him (Mark 10:46-52).

We are all like Bartimaeus. We come to Jesus blind to true reality, to the love of God for us. We cry for mercy. He hears, calls, touches, and heals us.

Throughout each day, we feel the need for God's touch and healing. We need his presence. That is why this prayer, usually in the form, "Jesus Christ, Son of God, have mercy on me," is so powerful. An anonymous Russian Christian in the late nineteenth century popularized the prayer as a way to "pray continually" (1 Thessalonians 5:17). For years this type of prayer has been common in Eastern Orthodox churches and more recently has been discovered by all kinds of Christians.

Begin by praying this prayer often during the day. It can be prayed inwardly wherever you are and whatever you are doing. It can be combined with the breath prayer, breathing in "Jesus Christ, Son of God" and breathing out, "Have mercy on me." If done often, the prayer will soon become habitual, changing our hearts and our lives.

Breath prayer, the Jesus prayer, and other brief, repeated prayers will keep us focused on God's love for us. In his book *The Practice of the Presence of God*, Nicholas Herman (also known as Brother Lawrence) called this "the habitual sense of God's presence," saying

> And I make it my business only to persevere in His holy presence, wherein I keep myself by a simple attention, and a general fond regard to God, which I may call an actual presence of God; or to speak better, an habitual, silent, and secret conversation of the soul with God, which often causes me joys and raptures inwardly....

In other words, unlike our relationship with others we love, we can communicate with God at all times. In silent prayer, by appreciating the beauty of nature, in all the events and daily tasks of life, and even with every breath we take we can constantly experience union with our God of love.

Reflecting on the Presence

Sometimes, however, we see the presence of God more clearly in retrospect. There are prayer practices that help us reflect on where God has been at work in us. One of those practices is a daily **examen**. As the word implies, this is an examination of our day, looking for all the ways God has been present even in the many distractions and tasks. Usually done at the end of the day, the examen raises the question of whether our actions that day moved us closer or farther away from God.

We might reflect on our day hour by hour. Did I begin the day with God? Did I have a time alone with him in prayer? Did I draw close to him even on my drive to work? Where did I see God active from 8 A.M. to 9 A.M.? Where did I lose sight of God? And so on throughout the day. To examine our lives this way takes courage and honesty. It means owning our feelings, whether good or bad.

The purpose of the examen is not to cause guilt—"I shouldn't have lost my temper then" or "I should have been thinking of God"-but to increase faith. It is to help us see how God pursues us every moment, always wanting a loving relationship with us. It is a way of listening to God's voice in the day past and turning our hearts to listen more closely in the day ahead. By seeing what God has done in us, we more clearly see where he is calling us in the future.

Another way we reflect on God's presence is **journaling**. Writing our thoughts and reflections on God can be a prayer. It is also a way of enhancing the other prayer practices we have discussed. One can write actual prayers, reflect on the experience of solitude, list those we want to lift up in intercession, discuss what we heard from God in Bible study, recount answered prayers, ponder beauties we witnessed—the list of possibilities for spiritual journaling goes on and on.

If you have trouble getting started with a journal, one suggestion is to make two columns on your paper. On one side list your thoughts, feelings, and experiences. On the other list what God is saying to you. In this way the journal becomes a conversation, both speaking to and listening to God.

What form should our journal take? That depends on our personality. Some write in prose, some in poetry. Some have an electronic journal, others draw pictures. Some write on scraps of paper, others have beautiful, elaborate journals. Again, do what is right for you. The important thing in journaling is to be honest and consistent in the practice.

A further blessing of journaling is to see the work of God in us over time. Like physical growth, spiritual growth is sometimes imperceptible. Remember when you were a kid and got tired of people who had not seen you for a while saying, "My, how you've grown." You couldn't see yourself growing because you were with yourself all the time. They could. Journaling allows us to look back at our spiritual life weeks, months, and years ago. By looking back, we can see how far God has brought us. God himself can say to us, "My, how you've grown."

Finding Your Own Voice in Prayer

As you consider the prayer practices discussed in these two chapters alongside others you may discover, you will find some that more readily open your heart to God. Give all these ways of prayer an honest try, then choose what works for you. Again, pray as you can, not as you can't.

When you discover the prayer practices that best communicate your love for God, you will likely put them together in a devotional form that is unique to you. That form may change from year to year as you grow in your relationship to God.

As an example of a devotional form, we give the following from Carl McKelvey, a colleague and spiritual mentor who adapted his daily period of meditation from several sources. It is a helpful model reflecting many of the prayer practices we have studied. It is not meant as a model for all, but as an invitation to discover your own particular voice in prayer.

A Daily Devotional

Father, I begin this day with the recognition that it is a gift from you. It is another day you have provided, and I will rejoice and be glad in it. I accept it with a spirit of thanksgiving, remembering that each moment is irreplaceable and holy, and must not be wasted on bitterness or self-seeking.

Dear God, this privilege I have of speaking to you as a son to a Father is also a gift from you—a gift made possible because of the sacrifice of Jesus. Just the thought of this causes me to shout your praise. You are holy God, the only God, God Almighty, and I pray that your kingdom come and your will be done on earth as it is in heaven. I ask that you give me food for my table and that you forgive my sins as I forgive those who sin against me. I also ask your help in my continuing battle with Satan.

May I this day find peace without want. I pray that I will overcome my craving for things—knowing that such demands are never ending and that life cannot be established on such a false foundation.

I will work toward treating everyone well. I will love them with no thought of reward. I will weep with those who weep and rejoice with those who rejoice.

Today, I will strive to be humble in demeanor as well as in thought, for I know that pride can warp my life. Because I know myself, I confess that I have nothing about which to be proud. My weaknesses and limitations cause me to face problems that often defeat me. Therefore, I confess my need for your help and the help of others—this help I will seek daily.

I will also work on developing patience. I will try to maintain a quiet mind in which your Spirit might work. I know there is value in silence in your presence and in the presence of others. May listening be my gift to those around me.

It is my goal to be less judgmental. This means I will be careful about the advice I give to others as well as any criticism I might make of them.

Because of my love and concern for family and friends, brothers and sisters in Christ, good works, and the world in general, I pray for the following. [This is followed by a period of petition for others by name].

And now, Father, it is my prayer that I meet you in your word. As I read, may I have "eyes to see and ears to hear" your word for me today. [A period of Bible study, using *lectio divina* follows. This year Carl is reading the same Psalm each day for a week, using a different translation each day.]

Finally, in silence I come before you and like Samuel I say, "Speak, Lord, for your servant is listening." [Silent, contemplative prayer follows.]

In this daily devotional that can be done in thirty minutes, we see Bible study, written prayers from Scripture, requests, thanksgiving, confession, lament, intercession, and silent contemplative prayer. In developing your own devotional, you too can benefit from these ways of praying.

Just Do It

Looking at all the prayer practices discussed in these two chapters may be a bit overwhelming. There are so many ways to pray! Again, one should not feel inadequate because one has not tried or has not mastered all these practices. We are all inadequate in prayer. We are all beginners. Remember that it is not learning to pray well or to pray better that counts, but only gratitude and surrender to the loving God who prays in us through his Son and his Spirit.

So try these ways of praying. Give them an honest try even if they are awkward at first. After a while you will discover what practices work best for you. Even that may change over time. We will talk about consistency in prayer and other practices in the next chapter. For now, the important thing is to pray.

For Personal Reflection

1. Are there times when you are already alone and silent? Perhaps at home, at work, exercising, driving? Could you intentionally turn those times into periods of silent prayer?

2. The Jesus prayer reminds us of our need for mercy. Where in your life do you deeply feel the need for God's mercy? Where do you need to show his mercy to others?

3. Are you often reminded of time throughout the day? Try saying a little prayer (perhaps the Jesus prayer) every time you look at your watch or hear a clock chime. After doing this for a week, reflect on how it has changed you.

4. Take a walk. Notice the beauty around you. Thank God.

Going Deeper

1. For twenty minutes each day, spend time in silent, contemplative prayer, perhaps using the centering prayer method. At the end of a week, ponder over those experiences of prayer.

2. Begin a daily or weekly practice of writing in a prayer journal. Use a variety of approaches until you find one that fits you.

3. Sometime in the middle of each afternoon, take just a few minutes and practice breath prayer. How does the practice affect the rest of your day?

Group Work

1. Discuss with each other what you find most difficult about your practice of silent prayer. Share ways you have found to overcome your difficulties.

2. In your time together as a group, spend ten minutes in silence. Afterward reflect on the quality of that silence. How is silence together different from silence alone?

3. Have members of your group who have kept a journal for some time tell about that practice and how it has helped them.

4. In your group, have a time to pray and ask God for a greater intention to pray. Ask for strength and discipline to carry out that intention.

For Further Reading

For Beginners

Peace, Richard. *Meditative Prayer: Entering God's Presence.* Colorado
    Springs: NavPress, 1998.

Reading Deeper

Issler, Klaus. *Wasting Time with God: A Christian Spirituality of
    Friendship with God.* Downers Grove, IL: InterVarsity
    Press, 2001.
Johnson, Jan. *When the Soul Listens: Finding Rest and Direction in
    Contemplative Prayer.* Colorado Springs: NavPress, 1999.
Keating, Thomas. *Open Mind, Open Heart: The Contemplative
    Dimension of the Gospel.* New York: Continuum, 1986.
Thibodeaux, Mark E. *Armchair Mystic: Easing Into Contemplative
    Prayer.* Cincinnati: St. Anthony Messenger Press, 2001.

Spiritual Classics

Kavanaugh, Kieran, ed. *John of the Cross: Selected Writings.* New
    York: Paulist Press, 1987.
Lawrence, Brother. *The Practice of the Presence of God.* Garden City,
    NJ: Image Books, 1977.
The Way of a Pilgrim. Garden City, NJ: Image Books, 1978.

CHAPTER SEVEN

Practices of a Committed Relationship

Falling in love is wonderful. Listening to the one you love, sharing your own inmost thoughts, and being together in silence are all thrilling experiences.

But what do you do when the thrill is gone? In every relationship there comes a time when the honeymoon is over and you have to face the reality of living together day by day. This time is not a lessening of the relationship, but a period of growing deeper. To love someone daily requires commitment. Regular practices display and sustain that commitment. You say, "I love you," daily. You bring flowers weekly. Twice a year you get away by yourselves for a romantic weekend.

The regular practices that sustain long-term relationships are many times extremely unromantic. You cook the meals every day, clean the house every week, pay the bills every month, and do the taxes every year because those are ways we concretely show love for each other. These regular jobs are not usually thrilling, but they are necessary for the good of those we love.

Disciplines and Rules

Relationship with God is also sustained by regular practices. The traditional term for these is **spiritual disciplines**. Unfortunately, "discipline" is a word that leaves a bad taste in our mouths. We associate discipline with punishment, perhaps even with being unloved. Or discipline calls up images of monks whipping themselves in their rooms, mortifying their bodies. Discipline sounds extreme, painful, and only for the spiritually elite. We may think discipline comes from guilt, implies that all bodily pleasure is bad, and produces the pride of being outwardly more righteous than others.

However, to be good at anything takes practice. Walking across a room, throwing a baseball, playing the piano, or reading a book—none of these actions come naturally to us. All had to be learned. That learning was many times awkward, painful, and time-consuming. But the rewards and joys of learning kept us faithful to our practices even when we did not feel like doing them.

It's the same way with our relationship with God. He loves us as his children. He initiated a loving relationship with us. Nothing we do can create or deserve that love. He gives it freely. Nothing in all creation can separate us from that love. But there are certain regular practices that sustain and deepen that relationship. They put us in the place where we can truly receive and enjoy God's blessings.

This is what we mean by spiritual disciplines. They are regular practices that strengthen, deepen, and sustain our relationship to God. As with all loving relationships, being with God is not always easy. It takes effort on our part. We must not exert that effort only when we feel like it. When something is important to us, we put it on our schedule. So also with God. It's not that he is only with us when we pencil him in. His presence is with us always. But regularly scheduled actions remind us of his presence and strengthen our constant awareness of God.

The usual term for scheduling these regular practices is developing a **rule of life**. "Rule" suffers from some of the same misconceptions as "disciplines." Rules may seem arbitrary. Following rules leads to legalism. "Rules are made to be broken," so we need not take them seriously. However, by rule of life we do not mean a system that we must follow slavishly in order to be right with God. Instead, "rule" comes from the same root as "regular." All developing a rule of life means is to choose those regular practices we intend to follow to deepen our relationship to God.

Keeping our rule is not legalism, nor guilt-based. It is being faithful to our commitment to pursue the loving God who pursues us first. As you try some of these spiritual practices, they may at first feel uncomfortable and unnatural. You may think you are just outwardly going through the motions. But give them a chance. Like all new skills, the more you practice, the more the actions come naturally. You even begin to enjoy them! This is the secret of the easy yoke Jesus promised (Matthew 11:25-30). What begins as an outward act changes us inwardly. We act our way into a new way of being. That's the power of the regular practice of spiritual disciplines.

Jesus and the Disciplined Life

Here, as always, Jesus is our example. No one was more aware of his relationship to God. Jesus is God's beloved Son. Yet, even Jesus knew the need for regular practices to sustain and grow that relationship. "And Jesus grew in wisdom and stature, and in favor with God and men" (Luke 2:52). For a long time that was a puzzling verse. How could Jesus the perfect Son of God grow in favor with God? It's not as if he were less God's Son when he was young and became more so when he was older. He was always the Son of God. However, he had regular practices that helped him grow in his awareness of what it meant to be the Son of God.

So it is with us. The practices never make us God's children. God chose us, adopted us, and allowed us to call him "Father" (Romans 8:15). However, we, like Jesus, need these regular practices to remind us of who we are and to deepen our experience of being children of God.

What regular spiritual practices did Jesus have? From his many quotations of Scripture, it is obvious he knew his Bible and had a regular practice of **listening to the word**. We already looked at his regular practice of **solitude**, of being alone with his Father (Luke 5:16). He had regular times of **prayer** and urged his disciples to watch and pray (Matthew 24:41). Although some didn't think so (Matthew 9:14), Jesus also **fasted**, beginning his ministry with a forty-day fast (Matthew 4:2). Jesus had a custom of **worshiping** with God's people in the Synagogue (Luke 4:16). He not only taught **service**, but also embodied it in regular practices, even washing the feet of his disciples (John 13:2-17).

Bible study, solitude, prayer, fasting, worship, and service—all regular practices of Jesus. As we engage in the same practices, we are simply following his example. However, as we discussed regarding prayer, our relationship with Jesus is more dynamic than that. He has not left us to follow his example on our own power. This is why many fail at the disciplines; they rely on their own strength. Instead, Jesus through his Spirit lives in us. He is still listening, being silent, praying, fasting, worshiping, and serving through us.

So although these regular practices take effort on our part, that effort does not come from us alone. God not only gives relationship, he sustains it by engaging in these practices in us. Lack of effort can keep us from them, but too much effort can also get in the way. We let go, place ourselves in God's hands, and regularly practice our faith. Even Jesus learned surrender to the Father through these practices (Hebrews 5:8).

Practicing Reliance on God

We have already discussed most of the practices. Taking time to listen for God's voice, especially in Bible study, is vitally important (see chapter four). Silence and solitude also open us up to the voice of God. The many ways of prayer and the particular forms of prayer we use regularly deepen our relationship with God (see chapters five and six). Later we will look at celebrating God's love with others in worship and dedicating ourselves to serve others as regular practices of God's children (see chapter nine).

Here we focus on two other spiritual disciplines. The first is **fasting,** abstaining from food or drink for a set time. Perhaps no discipline is less practiced and more misunderstood by contemporary Christians. Jesus assumes his followers will fast and gives them instructions on how to do so.

> When you fast, do not look somber as the hypocrites do, for they disfigure their faces to show men they are fasting. I tell you the truth, they have received their reward in full. But when you fast, put oil on your head and wash your face, so that it will not be obvious to men that you are fasting, but only to your Father, who is unseen; and your Father, who sees what is done in secret, will reward you.
> Matthew 6:16-18

Fasting is not for putting on a show of holiness before others, yet Jesus says, "when you fast," expecting his followers to follow his own example. The Bible does not consider fasting unusual, mentioning it over forty times. Moses (Exodus 34:8), Ezra (Ezra 10:6), Daniel (Daniel 10:3), Paul (Acts 9:9), Barnabas (Acts 14:23), other prophets (Acts 13:1-3), along with Jesus and others regularly fasted.

So why do so few Christians fast today? For several reasons. Our culture teaches us from birth that it is our right to have our desires met immediately. Fasting is particularly difficult for us who have never truly been hungry. That is why it is so important to recover this ancient practice, so we can stand against a culture of greed where too much is never enough.

Some may not fast because they don't understand the reasons for fasting. Fasting reminds us of our deepest hunger, not the desire for food but the hunger for God. If we mistakenly think God would never want his children to be hungry, we must remember the experience of Jesus while fasting forty days in the desert. When confronted by the temptation to turn stones to bread, Jesus remembers the following passage that describes God's treatment of his children: "He humbled you, causing you to hunger and then feeding you with manna, which neither you nor your fathers had known, to teach you that man does not live on bread alone but on every word that comes from the mouth of the Lord" (Deuteronomy 8:3, quoted in Matthew 4:4 and Luke 4:4).

Because God loved the Israelites, he let them be hungry. He even caused them to be hungry. The whole idea may shock us. Doesn't God want to bless us? Doesn't he want to fulfill our every need? How can a loving Father deny his children?

What truly loving father does not deny his children? Kids don't know what's good for them. On their own, they'd eat nothing but junk food. When I was a kid and refused to eat my supper because there was something I didn't like, my dad always had the same answer, "Let him alone; he'll eat when he's hungry enough."

It's the same way with our heavenly Father. We don't know how to be hungry. We hunger for all the junk foods of life—money, sex, power, recognition, happiness—instead of hungering for what is truly good and satisfying. God wanted Israel to hunger for him alone. Jesus had learned that lesson. Have we?

One way we learn that lesson is by fasting. Perhaps some do not fast because they do not know how. If you have not fasted before, it is probably best to begin with a partial fast. This might mean giving up a favorite food or drink for a specific amount of time. Fasting, of course, usually refers to a complete abstinence from food, but not from water. If you wish to attempt a complete fast, begin slowly with a twenty-four-hour fast from one evening meal to another (skipping breakfast and lunch). From there, you might try a longer fast of three days or so. It is best to break a longer fast with a small meal of fruit. Don't try to make up for all the meals you missed at one setting.

Always remember the purpose of fasting. If you are concerned about being overweight or about your appearance, or if you are ill, do not fast. This is not a weight-loss program. As Jesus said, do not tell others about your fast (although you should share with them the results of your fasting). Fasting should always be accompanied with prayer. One can spend time usually devoted to meals to being alone with God. The sole reason for fasting is to grow closer to God.

We have been using "fast" in the usual meaning of abstinence from food. One can also fast from television, from other forms of entertainment, from shopping, from sexual relations (see 1 Corinthians 7:5), or from anything we desire. It's not that these things are evil in themselves (just as food is not evil), but they all have the potential to distract us from our hunger for God.

As with all spiritual disciplines, for fasting to be an effective practice, we must repeat it until it becomes routine. Although we must start slowly in fasting (and in all spiritual practices), if we persist we will experience the blessings of relying on God alone to fill our desires.

Another practice that reminds us of our utter reliance on God is **confession** of sin. Indeed, fasting is often connected with repentance and confession (1 Samuel 7:6; 1 Kings 21:27; Jonah 3:5; Joel 2:12). Like the tax collector, we fall before God and cry, "God, have mercy on me, a sinner" (Luke 18:13).

We confess our sins to God but also to one another. "Therefore confess your sins to each other and pray for each other so that you may be healed" (James 5:16). It may not always be best to confess our specific sins before the entire congregation of God's people, but there should be someone we trust enough that we can be open about our struggles. Small groups that covenant to keep confidentiality and to lift one another up in prayer can assist us in this practice of confession and repentance.

Confession and repentance are not to focus on our guilt and sin but on God's grace. When we turn to God (that's what repentance means), he accepts us, forgives us, and changes us. That's why genuine repentance always produces the fruit of action (Luke 3:8). Fasting, confession, and repentance are no good if they do not result in service.

> Is not this the kind of fasting I have chosen: to loose the chains of injustice and untie the cords of the yoke, to set the oppressed free and break every yoke? Is it not to share your food with the hungry and to provide the poor wanderer with shelter—when you see the naked, to clothe him, and not to turn away from your own flesh and blood?
> Isaiah 58:6-7

What is true of fasting is also true of all the spiritual practices we have discussed. They are not ends in themselves. They are not badges of holiness. They are not ways to force God to do our will. God designed them to turn our hearts to him. If we truly have the heart of God, then all the disciplines will lead to serving others in his name. Service is an indispensable practice.

Developing Regular Practices

These are not all the spiritual practices. You may find others that are helpful to you. The question is, "How do we take the practices and make them routine and habitual?" This is called developing a rule of life. Again, rule here does not mean a legalistic checklist, but simply making our practices a regular habit. As with a physical exercise program, such a rule or routine must be tailored to the individual. You must find what times and what practices work for you—daily, weekly, monthly, and yearly.

Here is an example of a rule of life:

Daily Practices:
* Arise each day with the thought, "This day is for God."
* Spend time in meditation on Christ as I jog in the morning.
* Spend thirty minutes each morning in Bible study and prayer.
* Say the Jesus prayer every time I look at my watch.
* Have a brief, ten-minute Bible reading and prayer after lunch.
* Reflect on the day with God in night prayer before bed.

Weekly practices:
* Worship with my church.
* Serve breakfast at the homeless shelter.
* Spend one day resting in God's presence.

Monthly practices:
* Meet with my small group for study, prayer, and reflection.
* Spend a day alone with God as a spiritual mini-retreat.

Yearly practices:
* Spend one weekend in a group retreat.
* Spend several days in a service project.
* Spend one weekend alone as a reflection on the year past and the year ahead.

Again, this rule will not work for everyone. If you are a parent with three small children, someone who has just started a business, or a physician with a busy schedule, you will probably find it exasperating to keep a rule like the above. Instead, perhaps all you can do for a while is to carve out fifteen minutes of prayer and Bible study during the day, while using reminders of God's constant presence like breath prayer and the Jesus prayer. However, determining to pray regularly with children, customers, and patients would certainly be an appropriate part of your rule.

One aspect of any rule must be times of rest or **Sabbath**. In Sabbath, we share the life of God himself, who rested after creation (Genesis 2:2). In a world that bases personal worth on accomplishment, where being too busy is the rule, it takes great courage and trust to take time to rest in God. Sabbath rest should occur daily, in those times of solitude where we "waste time" with God. A weekly Sabbath of a day, or at least an evening, where we spend time with God, family, and others we love will help center us on what is truly important. God gave us Sabbath to remind us that he is the one who delivers (Deuteronomy 5:12-15). The success of our lives does not depend on our busyness, but on the grace of our Redeemer.

We can also experience Sabbath in monthly and yearly **retreats**. What is a retreat? It is a time to withdraw from our usual activities to reflect on our lives with God. We can retreat alone, in small groups, or in larger groups including entire congregations. A group retreat should provide a rhythm of moving into solitude and then journeying back into the company of others. Many Christian organizations offer a variety of retreats; a look on the Internet will acquaint you with these retreat centers. Jesus felt the need at times to be alone with his disciples. Retreats allow us as his disciples to accept his invitation to "Come with me by yourselves to a quiet place and get some rest" (Mark 6:31).

How does one choose what practices to include in a personal rule? Begin by asking yourself what practices will best move you to a genuine relationship with God. What practices fill a need in your life? Which ones might help you work on some spiritual deficiencies? Then decide what times of day are best for your practices. Are you a morning person or an evening person? Do you already have habits of physical exercise or personal time that can become spiritual disciplines?

What about places for your practices? It is helpful to choose a special **place** to be alone with God. Jesus talks about a private room for prayer (Matthew 6:6). It need not be an entire room, but merely a corner, perhaps with visible reminders—posted Scriptures, pictures, and other objects—of your intention to be alone with God. Or perhaps you have a place outdoors to pray. Jesus himself preferred mountains (Mark 6:46; Luke 6:12; 9:28).

The most important thing about a rule is not how many items it has, how long you spend in prayer, or where you practice. Most important is consistency. The rule should eventually become second nature. Just as we don't have to think about how to take a shower, brush our teeth, or put on our clothes (although at one time we had to learn all of these tasks), so eventually the practices in our rule will become second nature to us.

What about changing our rule? At first, we should be somewhat slow to change from a particular practice. We should give that practice a fair chance. After all, practice means keeping at something even when we find it difficult and boring. Sometimes one gets the full value of a practice only after it becomes boring and routine.

However, we should be flexible in choosing and continuing practices. After a while, it may be that a practice should be jettisoned and another take its place. One deeply spiritual man we know has changed his prayer practices almost yearly. However, we should make changes only after praying about them. Let God choose your practices. We should not be overly concerned and worried about finding exactly the right practices. The point is to be consistent in whatever set of practices we have chosen.

A Transforming Relationship

Remember that the point of the practices and of our rule of life is not to earn the love of God or to make ourselves spiritually superior to others. The point is to grow in our relationship to the

God who loves us so much. Every practice focuses not on our experience of spirituality, certainly not on our sins and inadequacies (although we will feel those deeply), and not on our own ability to grow. The practices focus us on God.

As we spend time with God, he transforms us into his image. When Moses went into the presence of God, his face shone brightly with God's glory (Exodus 34:29-35). One cannot see the face of God without being changed. In reflecting on this story, Paul applies it to all children of God: "And we all, who with unveiled faces contemplate the Lord's glory, are being transformed into his likeness with ever-increasing glory, which comes from the Lord, who is the Spirit" (2 Corinthians 3:18, TNIV).

Spiritual transformation is a gift of God through his Spirit. Spiritual disciplines do not earn or achieve transformation. Spiritual practices, however, do cultivate a life in which contemplation of God becomes habitual. It is in that contemplation that we are transformed. That transformation, like all growth, is gradual; the benefits of regular practices are not seen overnight. But we engage in these practices in faith, trusting that the more clearly we see God's face, the more we become like him.

For Personal Reflection

1. What kind of "practices" have you had in your life, such as sports, musical instruments, and drama productions? How did you feel about having to practice? Did you enjoy it? Why did you do it? How do these experiences affect your attitude toward spiritual practices?

2. Aren't we saved by grace? Do spiritual practices sound like earning our salvation? Should we have to make an effort to maintain and grow in our relationship to God? How is this different from legalism?

3. What are some of the usual things you do to maintain and enhance your relationship with your parents? Your friends? Your girlfriend or boyfriend? Your wife or husband? Your children? Do you do those things even when you don't feel like it? Why?

4. If Jesus was the Son of God, why did he need to grow in favor with God? What were the spiritual practices of Jesus?

Going Deeper

1. Try a fast of twenty-four hours. When hungry, take time for prayer. After the fast, reflect on the experience. Why did you fast? Did it bring you closer to God? Did it change the quality of your prayers?

2. Determine to spend one day or at least one evening each week doing nothing but spending time with God and family.

3. Do a search on the Internet on "retreat centers." After prayer, book a weekend retreat at one of the centers.

4. After much prayer, write your own rule of life.

Group Work

1. Your group should have already committed itself to strict confidentiality concerning what is said there. Now, as a safe place for confession, each person should confess a specific sin or temptation to the group and ask for prayer.

2. Share your rule of life with the group, giving reasons for what you have chosen. After everyone has presented a rule, the group should then pray that God will give each the discipline to keep the rule.

3. After trying to follow your rule for a month, confess to the group the challenges you have faced in keeping your rule.

For Further Reading

For Beginners

Ortberg, John. *The Life You've Always Wanted: Spiritual Disciplines for Ordinary People.* Grand Rapids: Zondervan, 1997.

Reading Deeper

Foster, Richard J. *Celebration of Discipline: The Path to Spiritual Growth.* San Francisco: Harper, 1988.

Muller, Wayne. *Sabbath: Finding Rest, Renewal, and Delight in our Busy Lives.* New York: Bantam, 1999.

Reference

Jones, Timothy. *A Place for God: A Guide to Spiritual Retreats and Retreat Centers.* New York: Doubleday, 1999.

Spiritual Classics

Chittister, Joan. *Wisdom Distilled from the Daily: Living the Rule of St. Benedict Today.* San Francisco: Harper, 1990.

Foster, Richard J. and Smith, James Bryan, eds. *Devotional Classics.* San Francisco: Harper, 1993.

Part 3

LIVING OUT GOD'S LOVE

God demands we have an exclusive relationship
with him. We are to have no other gods. However, our
loving relationship with God includes a community of
faith. Our love for God and our brothers and sisters also
moves us to reach out in service to others, inviting
them into relationship with God and with us.

---

pride – worship self

CHAPTER EIGHT

Rivals to the Beloved

Regular practices open our lives to the transforming power of God. "God has poured out his love into our hearts by the Holy Spirit, whom he has given us" (Romans 5:5). In that flood of God's love, we have joy, purpose, peace, and hope. We live in that kingdom of love where King Jesus reigns. We show his love to all around us.

What a life! What could possibly disrupt such a life? Why would we ever neglect those practices that put us in the position to receive God's love in us? And yet we do. We find consistency in spiritual disciplines a struggle. We get distracted. We so much want to love and follow God, but we have other loves. We begin to let our exclusive relationship with God slip away.

Loving One and Only

I first fell in love with the young woman who is now my wife during the summer. Because we attended different universities, I frantically tried to make sure our relationship would endure the months of separation ahead by exploring every possibility of personal contact. Unfortunately, these were the days before e-mail, and long distance phone calls were expensive. So, with diligence and love, I wrote her nearly every day and planned weekend visits (ten hours one-way) whenever possible. I did not want her affections to be "stolen" away. My efforts paid off. By Christmas of that year, I proposed to her and she accepted.

I quickly discovered that just because we made a commitment to marriage, it did not mean that our relationship needed less attention. Regular practices of commitment are necessary to sustain a romantic relationship, not only after an official engagement, but after marriage itself. As we committed our lives to each other, we were also promising to avoid other romances that would break our vows to one another. It would be unthinkable for me to be undisturbed if my wife chose to continue dating other men. Likewise, my wife has made it clear that if I ever became romantically inclined with another woman, well....let's put it this way, life would change dramatically and not for the better. And clearly, it was and is right for her to claim exclusive relationship with me.

This does not mean I cannot love others, such as friends, family, and co-workers. But it does mean that I have promised my wife an exclusive intimacy that places our relationship above all others, save one. Of course, that is our relationship with God. He must be our first love.

If we are going to consider our relationship with God to be above even that of our spouse, we begin to realize how important it is that we have an exclusive relationship with him. We also need to recognize those things that might pull us away from him. My wife and I have discussed certain rules that we have observed in our relationship so that it will continue to grow in intimacy. In our differing work situations, we choose not to be in private relationships with those of the opposite sex (for example, I have never taken an administrative assistant of the opposite sex to lunch alone). If a woman comes in my office, I always leave the door open. My wife and I have agreed never to complain about one another to others. We choose not to demean one another in the presence of others, even if intended in fun. We want to continue to "date" each other. These are a few simple ideas. But these and others are important if we are to continue to grow in love and intimacy.

A Jealous God?

God also wants an exclusive relationship with us. He will put up with no rivals. The Bible often calls him a "jealous" God. This is not the harmful, irrational jealousy that can destroy relationships, but the overpowering love of God that wants us for himself. Thus, it is proper that God is jealous of our affection and love for him. We have acknowledged him as our Father, our God, and he deserves our faithful and focused love.

"A jealous God" may offend us. An unhealthy possessiveness and selfishness turn the one we claim to love into an object of our possession rather than the object of our love. Jealousy can even involve envy of others because of their good fortune. Note the unhealthy self-focus involved in such thinking. Clearly, God is not jealous in this way. However, if we properly understand his jealousy for us, his deep love moves us profoundly.

We see the intensity of God's love for his own people in his words to Moses, "Do not worship any other god, for the Lord, whose name is Jealous, is a jealous God" (Exodus 34:14). God's very name, in this verse, calls for exclusive relationship. There can be no other gods, no other loves like that which we have for him. If Israel had only obeyed the first two commandments, how different their story would have been. They are simple teachings to understand. "Have no other gods before me," and "Do not worship idols." But Israel continued to fall short of honoring the exclusive relationship demanded by God.

We shake our heads in disbelief! How could Israel follow the pagan nations in worshiping idols made by human hands? How could they commit spiritual adultery with pagan gods when God had shown his power and faithfulness to them in so many ways?

How could they be so foolish to trust in an idol carved out of dead wood? But take that same piece of wood, turn it into strips of paper with large numbers and pictures of dead presidents on them and we find ourselves guilty of the same sin. We worship, pursue, and trust that which represents great value to us. The idol of the mighty dollar stands tall in many of our homes. It is tragic irony that we inscribe our idols with the words, "In God We Trust."

The whole issue of idolatry is one of trust. Do we trust God alone to care for us? Or do we need "God and..."? Is it God and money that bring us security? God and pleasure that bring us happiness? God and achievement that make us fulfilled? God and family that create joy? It's not that we want to break up our marriage with God. We just want to play around with others. If that seems far-fetched, then ask yourself, "What if I lost all my property, my job, my friends, my family? Would I still seek God and find security, meaning, happiness, and joy in him?"

In the movie *The Jerk*, a man, who through incredible luck had become fabulously wealthy, lost all that he had. As he walks away from it all, he stops and picks up a small object and claims that it is all he needs to be happy. As he resumes his walk, he continues to add other objects he needs to be happy, until he is so overburdened he can barely walk. Is this who we are? If so, we will never find the joy God desires for us to have in our relationship with him. "Why spend money on what is not bread and your labor on what does not satisfy? Listen, listen to me, and eat what is good, and your soul will delight in the richest of fare" (Isaiah 55:2).

God is a jealous God for our own good. Only when we learn to love him above all else can we find the security and peace that he offers. God is not jealous because he needs us. He is jealous because only in an exclusive relationship with him can we find true life, the life he wants so much for us.

An Example of Perfect Trust

One aspect of Jesus' life that set it apart from all others was his deep trust in his Father. This trust freed him boldly to follow God's will in his life. From the beginning of his ministry, when tempted by Satan to worship him and receive the kingdoms of the world as Satan's gift, Jesus proclaimed the foundational truth that guided his every thought, action, and teaching: "Worship the Lord your God, and serve him only" (Matthew 4:10).

Where Israel failed in the wilderness, so quickly falling in worship before the idol of a golden calf, the faithful Son was victorious, allowing himself to worship God alone. He found complete fulfillment in his Father. He refused to be guilty of spiritual adultery, and it cost him his life. In the final moments before his death as he suffered on the cross, he painfully uttered those words that summarized the nature of his abiding trust, "Father, into your hands I commit my spirit" (Luke 23:46). Was his trust wrongly placed? Hardly! Look at what God did through the faithful obedience of his Son. Will we intentionally develop such a relationship with God?

I say intentionally because a deeper relationship with God will not happen in the normal flow of our lives in today's world. Maintaining even a casual relationship with God is not possible without some effort. Our culture is ripping us away from an exclusive relationship of trust with our God.

Our economy relies on our discontent and constant desire for more. The multi-billion-dollar advertising industry creates "needs" that we never had before, filling our minds and hearts with growing desires and insecurities. A survey done not long ago asked Christians if they believed greed was wrong. Most agreed it was a sin. The next question asked if they thought "always wanting more" was wrong. This time, the large majority answered that there was nothing wrong with that!

But "always wanting more" is a definition of "greed". However, we don't see it that way. "Wanting more" is the American way! "Greed" sounds terrible. We know the Bible condemns it, calling it idolatry (Colossians. 3:5). Paul condemns, not being rich, but the desire to be rich (1 Timothy 6:10). When anything but God is the aspiration and focus of our lives, we are guilty of idolatry.

But what's wrong with wanting more? It demonstrates our lack of understanding of what an exclusive relationship with God provides. He is, indeed, all that we need. One foundational truth in our lives is that we are complete in Christ Jesus (Colossians 2:9). One who understands this can say, "I have learned to be content with whatever I have" (Philippians 4:11). Such contentment is an expression of trust in the one who created us for that very kind of relationship with him.

Moving Away from Idols

What can we do to deepen our faith in God and move away from the idols of our world? Let me suggest two fundamental things. First, we need to deepen our understanding of who we are in Christ Jesus. Without continuous experience of our blessings in Jesus Christ, we will keep being enticed by the things of this world. Secondly, we must identify those things that would draw us away from him and consider what we must do to break their hold on us. Both of these actions can occur only through the work of the Holy Spirit. However, he invites us to cooperate with him by making ourselves available for his work. This is the purpose of the spiritual disciplines. They put us in a place that allows the transformative work of the Holy Spirit in us.

Knowing who we are in Christ turns us away from temptation. When we do not know who we are, we open ourselves to Satan's attacks. Because he knew he was the beloved Son of God, Jesus withstood the assaults of Satan. He would not turn the stones to bread, for he was under the care of his Father, and his trust in God was the food that sustained his life. He did not have to throw himself from the pinnacle of the temple to test God's faithfulness and protective care, for he knew he was God's beloved Son.

When Jesus was preparing his disciples for his imminent death, he said, "I will not speak with you much longer, for the prince of this world is coming. He has no hold on me, but the world must learn that I love the Father and that I do exactly what my Father has commanded me" (John 14:30-31). Satan had no hold on or power over Jesus. Jesus was beyond Satan's reach because he knew he was God's Son and loved God more than his own life. We also are beloved children of God—he proclaimed us so at our baptisms—but we open ourselves to Satan's attacks when we doubt his love for us.

God chose us to be sanctified by the Spirit for obedience to Jesus Christ. This is a new birth into a living hope. This wonderful new hope calls us to specific action, which makes our new identity a powerful tool against the temptations of Satan.

> Therefore, prepare your minds for action; be self-controlled; set your hope fully on the grace to be given you when Jesus Christ is revealed. As obedient children, do not conform to the evil desires you had when you lived in ignorance. But just as he who called you is holy, so be holy in all you do; for it is written: "Be holy, because I am holy."
> 1 Peter 1:13-16

Here are helpful practices for embracing our new identity in Jesus Christ. First, we are to prepare our minds for action. We are to realize who we are and to what we are called.

Secondly, in order to prepare ourselves for warfare, we are to be self-controlled or disciplined. This discipline is expressed in those disciplines, or regular practices, discussed in previous chapters. Such regular practices lead us away from conformity to the worthless callings of our worldly desires. They reinforce our new identity, and remove the tug of those desires. We are holy, set apart for the purposes of God!   We have a new identity through new birth. We are now living stones being built, or formed, into a spiritual house which is to be a spiritual priesthood, offering spiritual sacrifices acceptable to God through Jesus Christ (1 Peter 2:6-11). God calls us to this joyful life of obedience. Because we are now God's holy nation, we are strangers and aliens in this world. We must avoid those sinful desires, which wage war against us, at all costs.

New identity is central to the process of spiritual formation. Without a new identity, the spiritual disciplines just become another way of worshiping self. The key to falling in love with God is recognizing our desperate need for a new identity, a new start, a new life. Only then do we begin to realize the inexpressible value of the offer we have in Christ Jesus to start over. Removing the false idol of self from our hearts and replacing it with Jesus Christ is the secret of the Christian life.

God's strategy for defeating sin in our life, then, is to focus on who God has called us to be. We died to sin in baptism. Thus, we are no longer slaves to it. However, as long as we focus on the things of this world, we will continue to think of ourselves as slaves to sin. Instead, we should allow the Spirit to control us (see Romans 6-8).

So, the Spirit of God leads us to focus on the purposes of God for our lives. The worldly things that cause us to sin have no place in the mind of the believer. The secret of battling spiritual adultery is intentionally walking with God's Spirit.

Spiritual Exercises to Claim Our Identity in Christ

How do we do this at a practical level? Many who believe they have been born again have never intentionally changed their thinking. They have not realized the wonderful blessings of a new identity. They continue to remain fixed on the things of this world. This is where the spiritual disciplines can be extremely helpful. As we have described them, they are spiritual practices that develop thinking and behavioral patterns consistent with the Spirit of God.

Think of the disciplines as a toolbox. Each tool has a purpose, and can help you do what you could not do by hand. How do I use the disciplines to help me claim my new identity in Christ Jesus? Clearly, the discipline of **study** is very important in this discussion. Engage in focused spiritual reading, both of the Scriptures and of godly authors who will deepen your understanding of your purpose and life in God's kingdom. Open your heart to a deeply reflective reading of Scripture, looking for ways to change your pattern of thinking. Meditate deeply on thoughts that remind you of your high calling as a priest of God.

Prayer also reminds us of our identity. Pray with the knowledge of who you are in relationship to God. Listen for his loving voice. Pray to him with passion. Claim your rights as a child, but submit your will to your loving and all-knowing Father. Spend time alone with God in silence, intentionally avoiding thoughts of the things of this world. Develop a godly vision for your life by seeking his desires for you.

Spend time with those who have a clear sense of calling in the Lord. **Spiritual friendship** is essential as we battle the idols of our age. Learn thinking patterns from great warriors of faith and listen to the stories of their victories against Satan.

Intentionally engage in **service** activities that demonstrate your identity as God's child. If you are a child of God, act like it. Do things for others in such a way that you receive no credit. Selfless living does not happen by accident. At some point, the believer chooses to live in a way that is worthy of his or her calling.

Identifying and Breaking the Hold of Idols

We must identify and form specific strategies to break the hold of idols. This is a difficult and sometimes painful process. We cannot do it alone. We need the help of the Spirit and of close, godly friends if we are successfully to battle Satan.

Satan knows where and when to attack. We need to be intentional in identifying our weakness and the conditions that lead to our falling into sin. "Each one is tempted when, by his own evil desire, he is dragged away and enticed. Then, after desire has conceived, it gives birth to sin; and sin, when it is full-grown, gives birth to death" (James 1:14-15). Our evil desire begins the process. We are then open to Satan's enticing, which leads to the unstoppable chain of events ultimately ending in death.

Identifying our weaknesses calls for painful introspection. While Jesus could say of Satan "he has no hold on me," most of us have so many handles to grab we are easy prey for the one who wills to destroy us. The process of spiritual formation includes identifying those things that lead us into sin.

After identifying them, we remove the behaviors that war against our souls. We rid ourselves of malice, deceit, hypocrisy, jealousy, and slander (1 Peter 2:1). We crave pure spiritual milk, now that we have tasted that the Lord is good. Peter is calling us to lose our taste for the behaviors of this world because we have found something much tastier—genuine relationship with the Lord Jesus. The behavior against which Peter speaks centers on selfishness. The things he lists are vices of the self-focused heart. If you are guilty of these sins, stop and ask yourself why. Almost without exception, it is because we are thinking of ourselves first.

Paul also provides similar listings of sins. In Colossians three, where he speaks of "resurrection" behavior, he calls us to put to death those things of our earthly nature: sexual immorality, impurity, lust, evil desires and greed (which Paul says is idolatry). He then adds another list of behaviors to avoid: anger, rage, malice, slander, filthy language, and lying. Why? Because we now have a new identity. These behaviors have no place in the kingdom. They rob us of kingdom life. They lead us to idolatry, the false idol of self.

These are the behaviors of a person living for self and none other. Consider sexual immorality, impurity, and lust. All focus on me wanting more. Lust occurs when I see something that is not rightfully mine and I want it for my own pleasure. But lust is more of a symptom than a cause. If I think that all is mine to consume, of course I will struggle with lust. I will automatically objectify everything I see that I want, and I will use my fantasy to realize my selfish desire.

Spiritual Exercises to Break the Hold of Idols

How do we practically attack the selfish desires we find in our lives? Remember the different spiritual disciplines available in the "tool box" of the kingdom. Study, prayer, and meditation are again helpful. But let us consider some other disciplines that we particularly need in the fight against sin.

"Therefore confess your sins to each other and pray for each other so that you may be healed. The prayer of a righteous man is powerful and effective" (James 5:16). Why are we to confess to one another? So that we can know one another's weaknesses and pray for God's strength to overcome them.

Confessional relationships are crucial to fighting the battle against patterns of sin in our lives. We need people who are close enough to us to confront us when we sin. We need people who will love us in spite of our sinful behavior and lovingly guide us back into kingdom life. My lifeline in recent years has been a succession of different groups of individuals to whom I can openly confess my sin. This is not something I would feel comfortable doing in the presence of a large church. Not everyone can handle the confidentiality needed for helpful confession. My first confessional partner is my wife. She is my spiritual hero and loves me enough to point out my sin (even though I do not enjoy her doing so). But there are other sins in my life that require the help of fellow Christians. In such a group, we can realize the benefits of the discipline of confession.

Journaling, I believe, is an indispensable discipline in the battle against specific sin. We have so little time for reflective thinking in our culture. Taking the time to evaluate our lives in the Lord is an effective way to discover sin patterns that continually cause us to stumble. We do not journal for posterity. Our journals should read, "If found after my death, if you have any integrity, you will burn this." We don't even journal for ourselves. This is more than a form of self-improvement. Journaling should be a form of prayer. God is reading. He is listening. He is forgiving. He is empowering us to overcome temptation.

We need to be honest to God about our struggles. Journaling has been extremely helpful to me in understanding myself. It has helped me find passages of Scripture that apply to specific sins. These become powerful weapons against temptations.

There are many different forms of journaling, and I do not know which you will find to be most helpful. Almost without exception, my students find it to be essential, especially in their overly busy lives. Many hate it for the first few weeks, but by the end of the semester, they have noted specific changes in their lives.

Fasting is also a powerful tool in the battle against specific sin. Fasting accompanies confession and repentance throughout the Scriptures. It demonstrates a willingness to turn away from the calling of the fleshly appetites to focus on the God who sustains us. We live in a world of instant gratification. Our flesh controls our spirits. If we are hungry, we walk to a vending machine and buy unhealthy food. If we are thirsty, a water fountain is close by. If we have a headache, we pop an aspirin. If we have an impure desire, the Internet beckons.

Fasting teaches us that our desires are not our first priority. It helps us break the power of our earthly appetites. As mentioned in the last chapter, it does not have to be the absence of food. Some need to fast from their daily reading of the newspaper. They allow that morning practice to control their thinking. They cannot think of "the things above" because they are overwhelmed with the problems of today's world. Others need to fast from sports. They have become so distracted by the mundane that they can no longer see the eternal. Fasting from the Internet for a time would be helpful to most of us.

Other disciplines might be helpful as you battle specific sins. **Simplicity** as a discipline is something that many of us need to help us conquer the addiction of selfish consumerism. **Submission** is a wonderful tool to help us break the need to control others. **Solitude** helps us break our need for the approval of others. Identify your idols, and intentionally attack each with a godly discipline.

I am not suggesting we battle Satan on our own. If that were possible, Jesus did not need to die for our salvation. Only with divine help can we win the fight against sin. The good news is that such help is available! Jesus died to purify us from our sins so that his Spirit might live in us. But the Spirit will not confront the sin in our lives without our cooperation. The appropriate spiritual disciplines, or exercises, allow the Spirit to do his work, convicting us of sin and sanctifying our lives.

God loves us more than we can ever know. His love for us is so deep that he will not allow us to love other things or people more than him. If we love others more, we cannot find life as God intends it to be lived. Idolatry occurs when we place anything before God. It leads to a living death. If we are to find life, we must identify the rivals that stand between God and us. At all costs, we must allow God to remove them.

If we will learn to love God above all else, it will not mean that we will love others less than we currently do. In fact, if we love someone more than we love God, we do not love them enough.

We are attempting to love them with our own resources, which are amazingly limited. If we love God foremost, then we love others with his inexhaustible resources of love. We no longer love others out of self-love. We love them as the children of God they truly are. In our new identity, we no longer see others from an earthly point of view (2 Corinthians 5:16). Everything is new. Because we now love them with God's love, they are no longer idols, but objects of his love. And we become ministers of reconciliation, rather than consumers of all and everyone around us. God's jealous love saves us from loving others less than we should.

For Personal Reflection

1. Who are you? How do you see yourself? Do you form your identity by the world around you or by God's word?

2. Upon whom do you depend for your sense of worth? What does this cause you to do?

3. What sins most often attack you? Have you ever stopped to consider what it is that triggers the thought process that leads to that sin?

4. Reflect on the sin that you see in others. What do you think causes them to sin? Can you learn anything from their behavior?

Going Deeper

1. List three sins in your life you consider most serious. Consider a specific strategy against each. Pray over the list and ask God for direction in defeating these sins.

2. What are your most beloved idols? Why are they so important to you?

3. Set aside a day to spend in a quiet, restful place. Study and meditate on the identity Christ gives you.

4. Start each day with an affirmation of who you are (Isaiah 43:1, for example). Try this for a week and reflect on the difference it makes.

Group Work

1. Discuss with your group a specific idol that tempts you. Listen to the wisdom of the group on how to fight that idolatry.

2. Discuss the difficulty of fully realizing the blessings of being a child of God. Help each other discover your true identities in Christ and discuss the consequences of living your new identities in Christ.

For Further Reading

For Beginners

McQuiston, John. *Always We Begin Again: The Benedictine Way of Living.* Harrisburg, Pennsylvania: Morehouse Publishing, 1996.

Reading Deeper

Thompson, Marjorie. *Soul Feast: An Invitation to the Christian Spiritual Life.* Louisville: Westminster John Knox Press, 1995.

Willard, Dallas. *The Spirit of the Disciplines: Understanding How God Changes Lives.* San Francisco: Harper, 1988.

Spiritual Classics

Fleming, Daniel L. *Draw Me Into Your Friendship: The Spiritual Exercises of St. Ignatius Loyola.* Saint Louis: Institute of Jesuit Sources, 1996.

CHAPTER NINE

With God and Other Loved Ones

God invites us into genuine relationship with him. As we fall in love with him, he allows no rivals, desiring an exclusive relationship with us. However, although we should have no other gods, our relationship with God is not an individual, private relationship. God invites us into his very life, which itself is relational. Father, Son, and Spirit are a unity of love. That life of love pervades all our relationships. Falling in love with God always means falling in love with people.

The Blessing of a Loving Community

As we live out our invitation to fall deeply in love with God, we accept his gift of community. God creates a true community of believers who die to themselves and begin to lose their fallen ideas of possessiveness. They give all for the good of the entire group. They want to be together, to eat together, and to praise God together. They devote themselves to prayer and to the apostle's teaching. God expresses his love by their love for one another and for all, and so they joyfully grow (Acts 2:42-46).

This is a wonderful picture of what the church should be. People cut to the heart by their own sinfulness, repenting and dying to self, receiving the Holy Spirit, and becoming members of a true community of faith in God. In light of all that we have studied in this book, it is essential that we understand the place and purpose of the church in God's plan. Too often, church has been a way of avoiding a deep, personal, and intimate relationship with God through Jesus Christ, instead of encouraging such a relationship.

Generally, church membership is understood as some form of "meeting and agreeing with doctrinal requirements" and remaining faithful to those. Usually, the central focus of such teachings has to do with what happens in the weekly worship assembly of that church. Sadly, at times, a personal relationship with God is not required or even encouraged. The church becomes an institution defined by its rules and practices.

Instead, as we consider the church from the perspective of God's generous love for us, a different picture emerges. God has created us to have a meaningful relationship with him. Thus, church is no longer an activity to meet the requirements of our religious needs. It is our very reason for being. This doesn't mean we have to be involved in "church work" all the time in order to live a meaningful life. Instead, "church" is the body of Christ of which we are always a part. Our very life depends on the spiritual nourishment we receive from participating in the life-giving blood of the body.

We must avoid the dangers of a private spirituality outside of the context of community. Such "spirituality" ultimately makes one less useful to God. The proper exercise of the spiritual disciplines will always lead us to a deeper participation in community, not to a spiritual elitism.

In Colossians, Paul says that Christ, in the flesh, was the fullness of deity in human form. We receive that fullness when we surrender to him. It is the power of God that raises us from the dead and renders Satan, who would destroy us, powerless. As

Paul then describes this post-baptismal, resurrection life, his focus shifts to community. We are to put to death those things which destroy community and put on the new self where there are no longer distinctions based on the flesh. We are all made new in Christ. We are now part of a community whose members relate to one another in an entirely different way. We are no longer using others for our own perverted pleasures, we are no longer lying to one another, because we are called to be a part of one body.

Paul calls that new life the "clothes" of Jesus Christ—compassion, kindness, humility, meekness, patience, forgiveness, and love. We can enjoy and demonstrate these wonderful character traits of God only in community. Jesus said the entire law consists of loving God with all our heart, mind, and soul, and loving one another. We demonstrate our love for God as we love one another with the transforming love of Christ. That love creates communities where the peace of Christ rules in our hearts, where the word of Christ dwells richly among us, and where there are continual songs of praise to God and songs of encouragement to one another. Communities where all is done to the glory and honor of Jesus Christ.

Is this possible? Apparently Paul thought so. But such a community begins with individuals hearing the call of God, surrendering their lives and falling in love with him. Loving communities of faith are built on the love of God, not the letter of the law.

We are each members of the same body, working under the direction of the head, Jesus himself. Ephesians 4:12-16 provides a complete picture of the church in action. Christ gave gifts of leadership in order to equip the individual members of the body for works of service. Every member is to come to maturity, to the measure of the full stature of Christ, so false teachings do not destabilize us. Instead, we live the truth to grow up into him who is the head, Christ Jesus. This growth results in true community, because every part is supplying nourishment by working according to its purpose. A growing body builds itself up in love. Love for God and love for one another are the identifying marks of an authentic community of faith.

For Paul, this was not some dreamy idealistic picture. He expected the church to function this way. If we are to recover the Christian community as an expression of God's love, we must turn away from today's tendencies to minimize our participation in community, and instead find ways of making such a sharing of life indispensable. This discussion is crucial, if we are to avoid the hyper-individualism of our culture. We cannot be authentic disciples outside of a genuine and loving community.

Community is an intrinsic part of God's loving plan for our lives. It is a wonderful gift from God to incite us, to spur us, to lead us to his feast. Community is where we test our growing love for the Father. We express our love for him by loving those who join us on our journey of faith (1 John 4:19-21). Consequently, we must not neglect attending assemblies (Hebrews 10:25). We all need the encouragement to live a life of faithful goodness, all the more as the day of Christ's return is approaching.

As we become authentic disciples of Jesus, professing our love for him above all others, we become a part of a loving community of selfless, God-glorifying people who form a functioning body. Each member has a purpose in that body, leading to deeper nourishment by the Spirit. As each part participates in the body through ministry to others, the entire body grows in maturity and love. The final test of authentic Christian community is love for one another (Ephesians 4:16).

In the recovery of authentic community we will find blessings that many contemporary Christians have lost. These blessings provide indispensable assistance in personal spiritual growth. They are the key to inciting authentic and dynamic growth in churches. True growth does not occur through increasing the numbers attending our services. It occurs through the personal spiritual growth of individual members within the context of genuine, loving community. Let us consider a few of these blessings of authentic community: worship, discernment, spiritual friendship, hospitality, and service.

A Worshiping Community

There should be no greater joy in the life of a believer than coming into the presence of God in the assembly of fellow believers. Of course, we are always in the presence of God. But in the history of God's people, there have always been special times to focus intentionally on giving God his worth, praising him for who he is, adoring him for what he has done, and anticipating what he is about to do. In those times, we are particularly aware of his presence and love.

The assemblies discussed in the New Testament reflect a joyful gathering for praising God for the blessings received through Christ Jesus. Trying to figure out exactly the right formula that would satisfy God is to miss the point of the assembly. He is not a God who needs us (Psalm 50), but he is a God who wants us. We need him! We need the worship assembly in order to remember that life is not about us. We come before him with the sacrifice of our lives and renew our covenant to live for his glory. So we lift our hearts in song and prayer, we study his written truths, we dine at his spiritual feast. We remember his magnificent works. We rejoice in our certain place at his eternal feast. Our lives are changed. And God delights in the submissive, worshipful heart.

Once at the end of a tiring day, my first grader peeked around the corner. It was past bedtime, but I could tell he wanted to tell me something, so I signaled him to come and sit in my lap. He placed his head against my chest and tenderly placed his hands in mine. "Dad," he said, "I just want you to know I understand what you are going through. Going to school all day is really tiring and hard! I am proud of you and I love you!" He gave me a kiss, smiled, and ran to bed. I can't tell you how different I felt because of his demonstration of affection and love. I was no longer tired.

Is that how the Father feels when we submit to him and place our lives in his care? I am not suggesting the eternal Father tires, but I do know he desires our love. I believe that if we would see worship as an opportunity to express sincere love to our loving Father, in the community of others who love him, our assemblies would always be life changing. God has always intended for worship to be relational, not rote religious ritual.

In the Corinthian assemblies, each believer had a hymn, a lesson, a revelation, or a tongue (likely a message in a foreign language that would need translation). Paul suggested they control this excitement so that it could be edifying and meaningful to everyone (1 Corinthians 14:26). Wouldn't it be wonderful to be a part of an assembly where we are so excited about our growth in the Lord during the week that we all want to share something? Note that Paul's response was not so much about the proper order or parts of worship, but results. Worship should be orderly so that all can be built up and encouraged.

Paul is attempting to lead the church away from activities that promote individual spirituality but do not build community. He is concerned that unbelievers would see all of the confusion caused by tongues and think the believers were crazy. Instead, if unbelievers heard teachings that were clearly from God, which in turn were deeply experienced in the lives of the believers (Paul refers to this as prophecy), they would be convicted. They would fall on their knees and say, "God is really among you." These assemblies experienced a true sharing of life-convicting truths from the Spirit of God. This sincere desire to be transformed by God had a tremendous impact on the lives of nonbelievers.

I have seen this dynamic at work. On Sunday evenings, I host a house church. As we discuss Scripture together, we make applicable life lessons. The members are confessional in their approach to Scripture. One night, a friend was present who had little or no belief. But he was deeply moved by the willingness to confess sins and by the earnest seeking for truth. When we later participated in the Lord's Supper together, we prayed for one another concerning specific sins that had disrupted our kingdom walk during that past week. God opened the heart of this man. He asked for prayers as well.

Paul spoke of this dynamic. There is always the danger of confusion and self-focus in the assembly of believers, and Paul's solution was to make sure that all was for the spiritual strengthening of the church and the glory of God. This focus moved even unbelievers.

When we speak of the worship assembly, there are endless questions about forms and acts of worship. But we need to ask the bigger questions, "Is this assembly deepening our love for God?" or "Is this assembly convicting us of our sins and transforming our lives by the power of the Spirit of God?" Some have suggested the way to recover genuine worship is to search the Scriptures closely and attempt to re-create the worship of the early church. However, even if we could do exactly what they did, word for word, action for action, if that worship assembly left us unchanged, it would not be meaningful to us or useful to God. If what we do in assembly does not affect our lives the rest of the week, it has little purpose.

The community comes together in worship to meet at the table of God, to be shaped by his word, to be fed by his Spirit, and to remember what God has done in order for us to be like Jesus in our daily work and activities. The actions of community worship are touch points of God's story of redemption. They are not actions that somehow fulfill requirements of worship; they are participative reminders of who we are. We lift our voices in song, joining the tens of thousands of angels in worship around God's throne now. We pray in community because of our intimate relationship with God, seeking his guidance in our lives. We gather at his table to be fed and led, remembering our story of deliverance, and anticipating the eternal feast in God's presence. We listen to teachings from God's word so that we might be formed and transformed by what is true. We give, not out of obligation, but because it allows us to participate in God's giving nature.

Rather than asking specific questions about actions and forms of worship, the better questions would be, "Do our worship assemblies allow God to change lives through authentic, life-challenging messages from his word?" Or, "Are we earnestly praying together, expressing our willingness to submit to God, and listening for his purpose for our lives? Are we singing songs of encouragement and praise? Are we dining at God's table? Are we learning to love him more? Are we, in ever-increasing measure, surrendering all of our life to him in worship?" These are the reasons we come together. We encourage one another to live in the real story of God's purposes rather than the temporary story of the material world.

Here is a personal challenge. I have learned that I can thoroughly enjoy and benefit from whatever assembly of worship in which I participate. It has not been easy. I used to be a worship critic, evaluating every moment from the perspective of my understanding and my needs. I repent. I no longer want to analyze worship. I want to participate in it joyfully.

This is where the discipline is helpful. I can choose to deepen my understanding of God's love even when the sermon is less than challenging. I can praise God with the very depths of my soul even when the songs are not the ones I would choose. If I prepare my mind for worship, if I ready my heart for an encounter with God in the midst of his people in that place, I am changed. A true, worshipful heart does not need a certain kind of preaching, a certain kind of song, or a certain dynamic of fellowship to have a meaningful experience of worship. All that is needed is an open heart and a community of believers seeking to please God in what they do.

I am not suggesting we shouldn't try to join a group with similar ideas of meaningful worship. I am just reminding us that worship is not about meeting our needs. It is about communing with

God in the assembly of fellow believers. It is about dining at his table. It is about learning to love him more. Approaching the assembly of the saints with this viewpoint allows us to see that the spiritual food is always good, whether it is exactly what we would order or not.

Group Discernment

One of the great blessings of community is the opportunity to seek wisdom through the collective discernment of brothers and sisters in Christ. Jesus promised that wherever two or three gather in his name, he will be there (Matthew 18:20). This is the promise of Spirit-led discernment among believers who gather in the name of Jesus. Our culture encourages us to make decisions for ourselves and to be independent of others. Individualism is rampant in our society. If we do not realize the blessing of collective discernment because of the noise of our culture, we will fail to receive one of God's great blessings.

Several years ago, I faced a difficult choice that would radically affect my family's future and my career. My wife and I were deeply confused over what we should do. So we assembled a group of close spiritual friends, of different backgrounds and different vocations, even including one with whom I seldom agree, and laid the situation before them. After an extended period of prayer, they began to ask questions and offer suggestions. It was an amazing evening. The Spirit of God was clearly present. Before the evening was over, my mind had cleared completely. With the help of God's Spirit through the collective wisdom of this group, I knew what I needed to do. Now, looking back, it was clearly the right choice.

In the past year, I have been a part of a group that meets weekly to pray with one another and to open our hearts to God. We begin with an extended period of silence, centering our thoughts on our walk with the Lord. Then, one at a time, we begin to share our personal stories. After each one shares his thoughts, we again spend time in silence, listening for God's voice in response to the needs of our brother. We do not try to fix his problems. We simply try to offer a word from the Lord.

This experience has been a profound one for me. At first, I was uncomfortable with the format. I did not like the long periods of silence. My mind was so used to quickly offering suggestions that I lacked the discipline of reflective meditation before speaking. What surprised me most in this experience was how different my responses were after a brief time of silence. In the quiet, certain verses buried deep in my consciousness came to mind. Thoughts that were profound enough to need quiet reflection were at my disposal. I can't begin to tell you how valuable this experience has been to me. I have received undeniably godly counsel from my brothers. This is the gift of collective discernment.

A closely related topic is the gift of collective discernment in the reading and understanding of Scripture. There is a possibility for dangerous, uninformed interpretations in such a setting, but the benefits outweigh the dangers. One community of faith divides into home churches on Sunday evening. Every week, they receive a study guide with Scripture readings and questions for each day. Each family is to discuss the passage and the questions. Then, on Sunday evenings, several families meet together to discuss the study notes provided with the passages for the week. At that congregation, discussion is not about football or politics, but about the life of Christ. Instead, they have profound discussions on the ways they have lived out the Bible passage that week. This is the blessing of group discernment.

Spiritual Friendship and Mentoring

"There is a friend who sticks closer than a brother" (Proverbs 18:24). Another of God's wonderful blessings is that of spiritual friendship. Many have returned to the ancient practice of "spiritual directors" and "spiritual mentors." We all have teachers. We have individuals who deeply affect us, whether we want to admit it or not. Our ultimate mentor, of course, is Jesus Christ. But he helps us on our spiritual journey through individuals we trust who clearly manifest the presence of the Spirit of God.

The purpose of mentoring is to bring individuals to their full potential as mature believers in the kingdom of God. When the Greek warrior Odysseus went off to fight the Trojan War, he left his young son, Telemachus, in the care of a trusted guardian named Mentor. The siege of Troy lasted ten years, and it took Odysseus another ten years to make his way home. When he arrived, his son had grown into a man of great wisdom, strength, and courage, thanks to the great teaching and training of Mentor.

Mentoring refers to the teaching of life skills through embodying the principles that are taught. Another word we could use is discipling. Some would suggest a difference, noting that discipleship deals with spiritual training and instruction while mentoring deals more with initiation and deepening in life skills. But there should be no dichotomy between the spiritual and secular realms. We are never outside of the interest and concern of God. I think our problem is that we have limited our view of discipleship. In discipling or mentoring, we walk through life with another so they can embody the skills and wisdom that we hold. And we hold those skills because we have learned at the feet and the side of Jesus, the ultimate teacher and mentor.

Note the shift from having a mentor to being a mentor. This is the beauty of true spiritual friendship. As you sit at the feet of one who truly exemplifies Christ for you, you become a mentor to someone who will sit at your feet. They in turn, will mentor another.

The greatest mentor invites us to be joined at the neck (take his yoke on us) and learn from him. The wonderful thing about Jesus is that all he teaches us he embodied. If we are going to continue to teach the life skills Jesus came to bring us, we need mentors, spiritual friends who embody truth as Jesus did. We then need to mentor others. In this way, we pass on the great story of the love of God.

Hospitality and Service

Hospitality has become the lost fruit of the Christian life. We have so centered our lives on our vocations and families that we seldom open our doors to anyone. Many families, much less strangers, no longer sit together for meals. We desperately need to recover the Christian graces of hospitality and service.

We truly worship God by showing hospitality to strangers, "for by so doing some have entertained angels without knowing it" (Hebrews 13:2). "Through Jesus, therefore, let us continually offer to God a sacrifice of praise—the fruit of lips that confess his name. And do not forget to do good and to share with others, for with such sacrifices God is pleased" (Hebrews 13:15-16). A life of intentional praise will take seriously the importance of hospitality and service of every kind.

Jesus constantly spoke of table behavior, encouraging us to get out of the habit of only inviting good friends and relatives to our table. He calls us to invite those who have no way of repaying us (Luke 14:12-14). In this way, we demonstrate our understanding of the nature of God's gracious invitation to us. None of us have anything God needs, yet he graciously invites us to his table. Will his grace leave us unchanged? We need to practice the discipline of intentional hospitality and open our table as God has opened his.

There is no greater example of serving than the life-changing story told in John 13. Jesus wanted more than anything else for his disciples to know the essence of his coming. He knew his time was short, he had come from the Father, and he was about to die. He took all the power of the heavens and demonstrated it in a shocking way. He took off his robe, humbled himself to the lowest of deeds, and washed his disciples' feet. When he finished his surprising deed, he wanted to make sure all of us who call ourselves his disciples understood the nature of his action. "Do you understand what I have done for you?" he asked them. "You call me 'Teacher' and 'Lord,' and rightly so, for that is what I am. Now that I, your Lord and Teacher, have washed your feet, you also should wash one another's feet. I have set you an example that you should do as I have done for you. I tell you the truth, no servant is greater than his master, nor is a messenger greater than the one who sent him. Now that you know these things, you will be blessed if you do them" (John 13:12b-17).

If God so loved us that he sent his Son to show us the way to kingdom life, we must not miss this profound truth. We show our love for God through our willing service to others. Unless we think we are greater than our Master, our Mentor, we need to rejoice in our calling to serve all whom we encounter.

So much more could be said about demonstrating the love of God and enjoying the love of God in community. We must not miss the point that falling in love with God means learning to love others. We willingly give our lives to our brothers and sisters and to strangers in hospitality and service, and we find the true blessings of Christian community in worship and spiritual relationships. This is how the world will know we are followers of Jesus, by the love we have for one another (John 13:35).

For Personal Reflection

1. How do you view the church? Is it a blessing or a hindrance to your spirituality? Why?

2. How can you contribute to making the church a manifestation of God's gracious love for us?

3. What new insight have you gained concerning the church as you studied this chapter?

4. Do you intentionally prepare yourself for the experience of worship in the assembly of believers? Why or why not?

Going Deeper

1. Reflect on God's plan for a loving community of believers who gather to learn more of his love so that they might love others more. How would this change your thoughts concerning church?

2. Identify someone to be your mentor or spiritual friend. Set an appointment with that person and listen to his or her wisdom concerning walking with God. Ask meaningful questions.

3. Identify someone you could mentor. Intentionally encourage them in their Christian walk.

Group Work

1. Discuss the idea of discernment with a group of caring spiritual friends. Explore the possibilities of sharing life's important decisions with such a group.

2. Intentionally host a "kingdom meal." Invite individuals you normally would not consider inviting. During the meal, gently invite them to fall deeper in love with God.

3. Discuss the importance of true service with a group of Christian friends. Set plans to offer meaningful service to those who need it most.

For Further Reading

For Beginners

Anderson, Keith and Reese, Randy D. *Spiritual Mentoring: A Guide for Seeking and Giving Direction*. Downers Grove, IL: InterVarsity Press, 1999.

Reading Deeper

Dougherty, Rose Mary. *Group Spiritual Direction: Community for Discernment*. New York: Paulist Press, 1995.
Wadell, Paul J. *Becoming Friends: Worship, Justice, and the Practice of Christian Friendship*. Grand Rapids: Brazos Press, 2002.
Webber, Robert. *Worship Old and New: a Biblical, Historical, and Practical Introduction*. Grand Rapids: Zondervan, 1994.

Spiritual Classics

Bonhoeffer, Dietrich. *Life Together*. San Francisco: Harper, 1954.

CHAPTER TEN

Inviting Others to Fall in Love with God

Falling in love with God is an exclusive relationship (we should have no other gods), but also an inclusive one. God includes all of humanity in his love. Jesus died for all, to reconcile the world to God (John 3:17; 2 Corinthians 5:15). God's will is to be done on earth as in heaven. The whole creation will be redeemed and renewed (Romans 8:21-23). God is near to every human being, drawing everyone into his love (Acts 17:27).

Evangelism as Life

God allows us who love him to join him in his work of reconciliation. Evangelism is one way of describing this loving work of God. Most believers, however, do not view evangelism as a joyous privilege. In fact, it tends to be a dirty word, not only in contemporary culture, but also in many churches. We know too many Christians who have twisted evangelism into a sales method or used it as a weapon to gain power over others. "We are the correct and only people of God, so join us (on our terms) or burn in hell." We also live in a time where tolerance means accepting all views as equally true and equally healthy. Even "Jesus" is a problematic word in today's world. A friend told me of a conversation she had not long ago with a Christian co-worker. She was speaking with excitement about the joy of walking daily with Jesus when her believing friend asked her to "tone it down." She explained that she believed in God and Jesus Christ, but the mention of the name "Jesus" made her nervous because it sounded so "exclusive." The name "Jesus" is offensive to those who consider themselves religious, but not Christian.

However, more than ever, the world around us needs to hear the good news of life in Jesus. We see the following Scripture reference at sports activities of all kinds, but its familiarity does not dampen its urgent message, "For God so loved the world that he gave his one and only Son, that whoever believes in him shall not perish but have eternal life" (John 3:16). Jesus did indeed make exclusive claims. As his disciples, we make exclusive claims—life in its fullest manifestation, life as our Creator intends it to be lived, is only in Jesus, the unique Son of the living God.

This indeed is good news. We have discovered the hidden treasure of the kingdom of God. We can now live in the end-time kingdom of God. By following the Son of God, we can find a life of meaning and purpose, a life that will never end. We no longer have to lead a futile and failing existence. And although the path is exclusively through Jesus, the invitation is completely inclusive, open to every person, no matter where they've been or where they are.

Yet many believers find it increasingly difficult to interest others in Jesus' call to salvation. Many place the blame on the rapidly changing world in which we live, often longing for an earlier age when we were more religious. The truth is such a golden age has never existed. The world has never shown an interest in pursuing God's design for life. But in every age, the proclamation of the gospel has melted many hardened hearts. The gospel is no less effective in today's world. It is as powerful as it has ever been. But until those in love with God live out the good news that Jesus came to offer us life in its fullest possible expression, the world will never have a chance to respond to God's invitation to love. How can they respond to that which they have not seen and heard?

The church still sees evangelism mostly in terms of methods and strategies, but effective evangelism does not happen through effective methodology, but instead through the authentic embodiment of truth. The mission strategy of the church is "The word became flesh and dwelled among us" (John 1:14). This was God's ultimate evangelistic strategy. He sent his Son to embody the truth of his love. Christian spirituality also embodies that truth. The entire biblical message shouts out with undeniable clarity that the kingdom grows through committed, genuine discipleship. We need committed disciples whose greatest desire is to know more about Jesus. That is what produces growth in the body (Ephesians 4:16).

Apple trees do not have seminars on bearing fruit. If they are healthy, they produce food for the world. Fish don't need workshops teaching them how to swim. It is the essence of who they are. Believers should not need training on how to serve the world from the spiritual table of God. It ought to be our natural response to the abundant love of God. But many believers see teaching others about Jesus as a burdensome task beyond their ability. This comes from a mistaken view of the true nature of evangelism and salvation.

This work is not easy. It is true that life in today's world is so complex and busy that people are not looking for one more activity to cram into their lives. If salvation is nothing more than attending church on Sunday, if it means that now I am obligated to another group with its set of activities, no thank you. But that is not the nature of the good news. If we truly practice what Jesus Christ came to give us, the life that results from springs of living water welling up within our hearts, we have a wonderful message of life that is amazingly relevant no matter where we find ourselves in the world.

It used to be that every time I met someone, I felt compelled to turn the conversation to something about faith or church as soon as possible. When invited to eat with new friends, we took them Bibles as house-warming gifts. Predictably, our friendships didn't last long. In fact, during one visit to a gifted artist whom I had befriended, he asked me how long we would be friends. I didn't understand his question. He clarified, "I am not interested in your religion. I have met people like you before. As soon as they understand I do not want to be a part of their church, they break their friendship with me." I assured him that our friendship was not contingent on his "obedience." However, it was not long until I lost interest in maintaining the friendship. His insight was deeper than I realized. I repent.

Embodied Evangelism

Amazingly, God worked through us in spite of ourselves and did some wonderful work that has endured. But what I wouldn't give to have those opportunities over. Since that is not possible, allow me to share with you five major truths I have learned about "embodiment-focused" evangelism. Each is discipline dependent. In other words, they will not occur without a commitment to consistent spiritual exercise:

1. God is already at work in every heart and every place. Our responsibility is to partner with him in such a way as to allow his power and truth to operate through us (Hebrews 3:1).

2. God works most powerfully through the servant who, with the help of God's Spirit, increasingly embodies Jesus Christ.

3. We cannot share what we do not have. The key to evangelism is an authentic relationship with God through Jesus Christ.

4. We must manifest a deep and sincere hope that is so apparent others will ask about it (1 Peter 3:15).

5. Communities of sincere love will stand as a beacon for those longing for meaningful relationships and purposeful lives.

Specific spiritual disciplines reinforce these principles. Here are some suggestions, but you will likely need to find your own pace and spiritual exercises in order to activate these principles in your life. A healthy body will grow, working according to its intended purpose to the glory of God (Ephesians 4:15-16). There are no shortcuts here. There are no quick and easy ways of convincing people to make a radical change in their lives. The key to numerical growth is the continual spiritual growth of every member within a community of faith. The community of God's people grows wider only as it grows deeper.

One of the most accurate markers of authentic spiritual growth is that it turns one outward, not inward. One who is truly growing in relationship with Christ Jesus will also take on Christ's passion for the lost. Another way of saying this is to say, "One who is learning to love Jesus more deeply will demonstrate it by loving those whom Jesus loves." Read the gospels. Why did the Pharisees so disapprove of Jesus? Much of it was because of whom Jesus chose to love. It was a radical departure from those of the religious establishment.

Consider with me each of these five principles and pray for guidance in letting them become a part of who you are.

1. God is already at work in every heart and every place.

This is wonderful news because it means our ability to reach is not dependent on our ability to teach. God is at work and has counted us worthy to be working with him. Will we be faithful to his call? Our responsibility is to be faithful workers in the field, to plant the seed. God will bring about the harvest (Mark 4:26-28).

The kingdom of God is like a mustard seed. It might be tiny when planted, but the Master will make it grow into a large shade tree that will comfort many (Matthew 13:31-32).

Our responsibility in evangelism is to partner with God and constantly place ourselves at his disposal. This does not mean we do not plan. There is clearly a place for planning and strategy. But God has a plan as well. "We are God's workmanship, created in Christ Jesus to do good works, which God prepared in advance for us to do" (Ephesians 2:10). The more we look for God's active work, the more effective we will be in proclaiming the kingdom. There is not enough room in this book to tell all of the stories of God's active participation in my life in presenting opportunities to teach I never expected. I cannot call it coincidence. God is the great "I am," not the great "I was." We have the promise that he will be with us, through his Son and through his Holy Spirit, until the end of time.

Disciplines to Help

One of the most helpful disciplines in the Christian life is morning spiritual exercises. Here are some suggestions for **morning devotions**. Adapt them to your own situation.

Each morning wake up with the thought, "My only reason to live is to live as if Jesus were in my place." Recite Luke 6:40 aloud, "A disciple, when he is fully trained, will be like his master." Meditate on Isaiah 43:1, a wonderful verse of reassurance, originally given to Israel as a call to hope, even after their experience of exile. "Fear not, for I have redeemed you. I know you by name, and you are mine." Isn't that wonderful? The God who knows the stars and calls them by name every night also knows our names. He redeemed us. He has a purpose for our lives. There is no reason to fear. We are his.

These thoughts place us in another world. We no longer live in the world of our own making, but in the world of God's incredible power and glory. Of course we are not equal to the task (2 Corinthians 2:16), but it is not about us. We are called to be the aroma of Christ wherever we go. Life has meaning and purpose. We are on a mission with God, every day, to represent his kingdom in every way we can. And God is faithful. He will do his work.

Another practice is to imagine ourselves putting on the "clothes" of Jesus—kindness, compassion, a generous spirit, and love—as we dress each morning. We need to do this intentionally, or we soon forget the true purpose of life.

Throughout the day, we also need regular reminders of who we are. **Regular times of quiet** help us refocus on God's direction. Before we begin a task at work, we ask God to open our ears to his word and our hearts to his work.

Not only do these practices change the direction of the day, they are also an intrinsic part of the amazingly good news of the gospel. Every person's life has meaning in the kingdom of God. All are looking for significance and purpose. I will never forget a rice field worker from India who was listening as I spoke of the kingdom. I knew nothing of his life in mud and dung huts. What could I say? "Repent, and hear the good news," I said, "God has a purpose for your life. You are light, leaven, and salt. All are of equal value in the kingdom." I watched this man with a toothless mouth open it wide in joy and wonder. He began to laugh, but not to make fun. He had never thought his life could mean anything. But in God, every living human being has infinite worth and wonderful purpose.

God is active. He is wonderful. He is the hope of the world. He is the Father of all and created every one of his children to his glory. It is to that truth we call all of humanity, whether in the impressive buildings on Wall Street or the slums of Calcutta. And it is a truth that we must not forget.

2. God works through servants who embody Jesus Christ.

If we want to lead others to truth, we, like our Lord before us, must embody the truth. We are all works in process, recovering jerks who can fall back into that behavior at any given moment.

And that self-focused, non-kingdom behavior is devastating to God's intent for us. The principle of embodied service has a negative and a positive side to it. There are things we must get rid of and things we must pursue (see Colossians 3 and Ephesians 4:17-5:20). There are things we must cultivate in our lives and other things we must remove. If we want to be effective proclaimers of the truth of Jesus, our lives must be consistent with that truth.

The teachings of Jesus were not mere sayings. His teachings were not aspirations. He first lived what he subsequently taught. People often remarked when they heard him speak, "He speaks with such authority." Indeed. He lived what he taught. In a word, he was the embodiment of truth.

"For you were once darkness, but now you are light in the Lord. Live as children of light (for the fruit of the light consists in all goodness, righteousness and truth) and find out what pleases the Lord" (Ephesians 5:8). Note the final phrase "find out what pleases the Lord." If we would all live to that calling, evangelism would be natural. We know that God desperately wants everyone to find the truth of Jesus. All of heaven rejoices when the sinner repents and comes home. We have the wonderful privilege of being God's agents of reconciliation (2 Corinthians 5). But until we live the truth we claim to pursue, the world cannot see the light.

Disciplines to Help

Intentional embodiment of truth calls for many of the classic disciplines. **Study, meditation, contemplation,** and **prayer** are indispensable aids for this pursuit. Particularly helpful but also painful is honest **journaling**. We need to recognize our failures of embodiment so that we can intentionally attack the tools Satan is using to distract us.

Confession is also indispensable if we are to live truthfully. We will continue to fall, perhaps often. But when we fall, we need to face the responsibility of our actions and do all we can to make the situation right. Authentic disciples do not live without sin, but when we sin, we are quick to confess that sin and ask forgiveness. We also are quick to accept that forgiveness, forgiving ourselves and releasing our guilt so we can continue to be reconciling.

3. We cannot share what we do not have.

The key to successful evangelism is an authentic relationship with God through Jesus Christ. This is the most prominent reason for the failure to teach the world about Jesus. The world sees little of Jesus in us because there is little of Jesus in us. We have not allowed him to do his transforming work because we do not have a relationship profound enough to allow that change to occur. We do not see it in ourselves, so we do not expect it of others.

We cannot walk daily with Jesus and remain as we are. It is impossible. Walking with Jesus will make deep and lasting changes that will be undeniable to those who know us. But if we do not have a meaningful, personal, transforming relationship with God through Jesus, we cannot lead others to it. We should be so thankful for the reality of Jesus that we are compelled to call others to him (1 John 1:1-4).

Are we this excited about our walk with Jesus? If not, no wonder we struggle with evangelism. What is our message? Come to church and be bored with me? That is not very compelling. But if you believe you are walking daily with the very Author of life, and you are learning how to glorify the God who created you, listening to the voice of his Son, how can you not share it with others?

Disciplines to Help
Walking with Jesus today is an intentional choice. Jesus told his disciples that he would not leave them alone. He would leave another comforter to lead them in the way they should go (John 14-16). Paul tells us that the secret to living the kingdom life is walking with the Holy Spirit (Romans 8). But how do we walk with the Spirit?

Once again, the basic disciplines are essential. One cannot be led by the Spirit if not fed by the Spirit, regularly and intentionally.

Dedicate time to relational **reading**. Intentionally place Jesus in the room with you as you read of him. Train yourself to stop at crucial times and ask for guidance from the Spirit when confronted with difficult choices. Train your thinking so that you develop a "missional ethic." That is, you make decisions based on whether your action will advance or impede the cause of Christ in you. Practice **prayer** without ceasing (1 Thessalonians 5:17), intentionally choosing to walk with Jesus in everything that you do. Consider the discipline of **submission**, willingly placing yourself at the call of others and of God.

If we are to show to others a meaningful relationship with God, we must organize our lives around activities that allow us to grow closer to our Lord. A relationship does not deepen without much time dedicated to that purpose.

4. We must manifest a hope so apparent that others will ask about it.

As obvious as the first three principles have been, these last two call us to consider things that may make us uncomfortable. Yet, we desperately need them if we are to be light to the world. Scripture continually calls us to hope. This is not a "hope" that continually wavers. It is a confident hope of that which is yet to come. We should know the end of the story (Act Six, remember?). Jesus is coming again, and he will make everything new. He will bring justice. He will bring right judgment. He will vindicate those treated wrongfully. Truth will prevail, the kingdom will come, and we will reign with God forever.

Do we believe Jesus is coming? If we do, it has two major implications. First, the world situation will not overwhelm us. Jesus overcame the world (John 16:33). Ultimately, we have no worries because we are living in his care. Secondly, God is even now bringing in his kingdom of peace and justice.

One of the great hindrances to evangelism has been our lack of involvement in righting social wrongs. Biblical hope does not lead us away from our concern for injustices in our world. It calls us to work at overcoming them. After all, if we believe Jesus is coming again for that purpose, how can we not be about his work now? If we know God is concerned for the poor, how can we not be involved in feeding them? If we know that Jesus came to set the oppressed free, should we not be involved as well in his work? We marvel that he cast out demons, but we quietly allow Satan's work to continue in the world around us. Should we not be involved in defeating Satan's work as Jesus was?

Peter believed the hope of the Christian would cause others to question the basis for it. "But in your hearts set apart Christ as Lord. Always be prepared to give an answer to everyone who asks you to give the reason for the hope that you have. But do this with gentleness and respect, keeping a clear conscience, so that those who speak maliciously against your good behavior in Christ may be ashamed of their slander" (1 Peter 3:15, 16). This powerful passage calls us to certain disciplines.

Setting apart Jesus as Lord in our hearts changes everything. It gives us a completely new outlook on life. Through prayer, study, and contemplation, we need to be constantly allowing the Spirit of God to dethrone our egos so that Jesus can act as Lord of our lives. Then we no longer fear what the world fears. We do not fear those who can kill the body. We instead have a deep, reverential fear for God. World events cannot worry us. Nothing fundamentally changed on 9/11 for the believer. For those who trusted in the security of our nation things changed dramatically. For those who trust in the eternal Lord and have their hope fully on him, nothing changes.

This does not make us unconcerned about violence and injustice. In fact, it does the opposite. It calls us to engage in things God would have us do. We pray for those who lose dear ones. We give to those in need. We work for peace. We do not take vengeance, for we can leave that to the Lord, as Paul commanded, "Do not repay anyone evil for evil. Be careful to do what is right in the eyes of everybody. If it is possible, as far as it depends on you, live at peace with everyone. Do not take revenge, my friends, but leave room for God's wrath, for it is written: 'It is mine to avenge; I will repay,' says the Lord. On the contrary: 'If your enemy is hungry, feed him; if he is thirsty, give him something to drink. In doing this, you will heap burning coals on his head.' Do not be overcome by evil, but overcome evil with good" (Romans 12:17-21). Outside of hope in Christ Jesus, such behavior is nonsensical.

Disciplines to Help
The first discipline to help us in this area is **discernment**. We must not close our eyes to pain, poverty, violence, and injustice. We must train ourselves to look beyond the borders of our communities and our nations to see the mighty hand of God at work. We should read and watch media stories of injustice, but realize that those accounts are slanted by self-interest, capitalism, and nationalism. Through Scripture reading, prayer, and group discernment, we will increasingly develop the heart of God, a heart full of compassion for the oppressed. But we cannot help the poor if we refuse to see them.

Discernment also allows us to hear God's specific call to us. We cannot help everyone in need. We must learn when to say, "Yes," and when to say, "No," to specific requests for our time and money. We will avoid compassion burnout only if we allow God to guide us and empower us for service.

Secondly, we need to act, to serve the world in hope. This will include political action, since God rules over every nation through his kingdom. God's politics are not those of self-interest, or the power politics of a representative democracy. They are the politics of unselfish love and **service** even to our enemies. In a time of fear, distrust, and violence, we proclaim the Prince of Peace who calls us to protest, to non-violent resistance, and to prayer.

We are also called to specific acts of service. Volunteer at a homeless shelter. Teach prisoners. Donate money and time to a food bank. We can serve the neighbor in our communities in countless ways.

Our role is to give the world the hope that we have. So when we see injustice, we want to do that which is right. When we see hunger, we want to share the goodness with which we have been blessed. When we see oppression, we call out to our God who can deliver and we do all we can to advance his kingdom by standing against all forms of injustice.

5. Communities of sincere love will stand as a beacon for those longing for meaningful relationships and a purposeful life.

Clearly, the church plays a crucial part in God's plan to evangelize the world. However, the role of the church in evangelism is not what we have commonly thought. None would suggest the church should not be evangelistic in some form. The question is, "To what extent must the church be involved in evangelism in order to be faithful to God's calling?" The answer—the only purpose of the church is to be missional. Missional is a word recently coined to identify the very heart of God. God has a mission. We are his children. We must be about his mission. It is our only reason for being.

God's mission is to reconcile the world to himself in love. He has chosen to do this through the church. "[God's] intent was that now, through the church, the manifold wisdom of God should be made known to the rulers and authorities in the heavenly realms, according to his eternal purpose which he accomplished in Christ Jesus our Lord" (Ephesians 3:10-11). The church makes God's incredible wisdom known to the evil forces that would destroy his work. What an amazing calling!

We must be ambassadors of the kingdom of God. We must demonstrate a love for one another that overcomes the powers that would destroy us. We are concerned for the fallen nature of the world. We should be communities of faith, meeting the spiritual and physical needs of those around us. Why? Because Jesus has destroyed Satan and his lie that life is about getting all we can for ourselves.

The church must be about being the people who manifest the power of God in their lives. If we do not love one another, forgive one another, and care for one another, if we are not the first to respond to the tragedies in our world in a meaningful, generous, and loving way, how will people know of our loving God?

Disciplines to Help

Now we speak of corporate disciplines, not just individual. Each community of faith must take an intensive look at its identity. For what are we known? What could we do to manifest the love of God in a meaningful way? Are we willing to **fast** in order to send food to those who need it? Will we engage in a **lament** for the fallen nature of our world? Will we lay our lives before the Lord and ask him to guide us as his people to be concerned over those things that concern him?

One discipline here is **hospitality**. As church we must make all people welcome in our places of worship and our homes. The cars we drive, the houses we have, and the clothes we wear all say, "You are not welcome," to the homeless, addicted, and poor. We must literally invite them in. Eat with them. Serve them. Genuinely befriend them. This is the heart of God.

God's love does not stop with us. If we allow it to, we have not understood it. His love is inexhaustible. He calls us by his love to make his love known to the world around us. We cannot be passionately in love with God and not be concerned with that which is closest to his heart. We will be evangelistic as a church when we draw near to God's heart, and, in the context of an authentic relationship with him, we take up his cause in this dark world. The light is come. Let it shine.

For Personal Reflection

1. What is your view of evangelism? Do you feel a personal call to this? Why or why not?

2. What must we do to recover the biblical call to share the good news of the kingdom with the world?

3. Why do you think we have not been very effective in sharing the gospel? What can we do to change this?

Going Deeper

1. What is the best news you know? How can you make the reality of the kingdom the focus of your life?

2. Intentionally start the day with a reminder of God's purpose for your life. Reflect how this changes even the mundane activities of your day.

3. What do you need to do to take on Jesus' passion for the world? Identify those things in your life that cause you to be apathetic to this passion.

4. Do you have something of great value to share with the world? Carefully consider what you understand the gospel to be and what you need to do to share it with those with whom you are closest.

Group Work

1. Consider ways you can encourage your congregation to focus on its call to share the good news. Find others who have your passion and pray that God would lead you to effective ways of authentic proclamation of the truth.

2. Consider ways of being more intentional in embodying truth as a community of faith.

3. What are ways you can demonstrate to those around the location of your community of faith that you have a deep love and concern for them and their needs?

4. Consider experiencing a fast as a church to better understand God's calling for you in the place where you are.

For Further Reading

For Beginners

Hollyday, Joyce. *Then Shall Your Light Rise: Spiritual Formation and Social Witness.* Nashville: Upper Room Books, 1997.

Reading Deeper

Camp, Lee, *Mere Discipleship: Radical Christianity in a Rebellious World.* Grand Rapids: Brazos Press, 2003.

Kenneson, Philip D. *Life on the Vine: Cultivating the Fruit of the Spirit in Christian Community.* Downers Grove, IL: InterVarsity Press, 1999.

Vennard, Jane. *Embracing the World: Praying for Peace and Justice.* San Francisco: Jossey-Bass, 2003.

Webber, Robert E. *Ancient-Future Evangelism: Making Your Church a Faith-Forming Community.* Grand Rapids: Baker, 2003.

Willard, Dallas. *Renovation of the Heart: Putting on the Character of Christ.* Colorado Springs: NavPress, 2002.

Spiritual Classics

O'Connor, Elizabeth. *Journey Inward, Journey Outward.* New York: Harper and Row, 1968.

Conclusion

Falling in love is frightening. The breathing gets short, the heart pounds, the mind reels as we imagine the depth of commitment it takes to maintain a lasting relationship. If we begin to contemplate marriage after only five or six dates, we shouldn't be surprised if we get scared. We simply are not ready.

It may be that after reading this book you are frightened, overwhelmed by different ways to hear God, speak to him, and have relationship with him. The depth of commitment required for that relationship might scare you away. Who can find the time or energy for these practices?

On the other hand, you might think the suggestions in the book are great and are really something you should do. Just not yet. Someday when things calm down, when you've grown spiritually, and when it's more convenient, you'll begin an intentional program of spiritual development.

Two words are key to those who have read this book, "Start" and "Trust." Start. Start small. Begin with ten minutes each day, at a time best for you. In those ten minutes, read a brief Bible verse and pray. Keep it up daily for several weeks. After this time becomes a habit, expand into other ways to hear God and pray. Perhaps increase your time. Don't just read this book. Do something. Start!

But we can only start if we trust. The writers of this book have written much better than we practice. We also have only started. Yet we are convinced that even with our feeble efforts, God is at work in us. Spiritual growth is an act of pure faith. We cannot always see God at work in our lives. It seems at times he's doing nothing. It even looks as though we are moving backwards in our spiritual journey. But no matter how it seems or looks, we come to God in faith, trusting that he is certainly but slowly shaping us into the image of Jesus. We believe his Spirit works in us, even when we cannot feel him.

Start. Start small. Start in trust. God will reward the briefest attempt to accept his love. God produces great plants from the smallest seeds. Begin today, as God's beloved child. He is pleased with you.

> How great is the love the Father has lavished on us, that we should be called children of God! And that is what we are! The reason the world does not know us is that it did not know him. Dear friends, now we are children of God, and what we will be has not yet been made known. But we know that when he appears, we shall be like him, for we shall see him as he is. Everyone who has this hope in him purifies himself, just as he is pure.
> 1 John 3:1-3